READING
EXPLORER

THIRD EDITION

1

NANCY DOUGLAS

DAVID BOHLKE

NATIONAL GEOGRAPHIC

LEARNING

Australia · Brazil · Mexico · Singapore · United Kingdom · United States

NATIONAL GEOGRAPHIC
LEARNING

National Geographic Learning,
a Cengage Company

Reading Explorer 1
Third Edition

Nancy Douglas and David Bohlke

Publisher: Andrew Robinson

Executive Editor: Sean Bermingham

Associate Development Editor: Yvonne Tan

Director of Global Marketing: Ian Martin

Heads of Regional Marketing:

Charlotte Ellis (Europe, Middle East and Africa)

Kiel Hamm (Asia)

Irina Pereyra (Latin America)

Product Marketing Manager: Tracy Bailie

Senior Production Controller: Tan Jin Hock

Associate Media Researcher: Jeffrey Millies

Art Director: Brenda Carmichael

Operations Support: Hayley Chwazik-Gee

Manufacturing Planner: Mary Beth Hennebury

Composition: MPS North America LLC

For permission to use material from this text or product, submit all requests online at **cengage.com/permissions**
Further permissions questions can be emailed to
permissionrequest@cengage.com

Student Book with Online Workbook:
ISBN-13: 978-0-357-12351-5

Student Book:
ISBN-13: 978-0-357-11625-8

National Geographic Learning
20 Channel Center Street
Boston, MA 02210
USA

Locate your local office at **international.cengage.com/region**

Visit National Geographic Learning online at **ELTNGL.com**
Visit our corporate website at **www.cengage.com**

Printed in China
Print Number: 01 Print Year: 2019

CONTENTS

Scope and Sequence   4

Introduction   6

Unit 1:   **Amazing Animals**   7

Unit 2:   **Travel and Adventure**   21

Unit 3:   **The Power of Music**   35

Unit 4:   **Into Space**   49

Unit 5:   **City Life**   63

Unit 6:   **Backyard Discoveries**   77

Unit 7:   **When Dinosaurs Ruled**   91

Unit 8:   **Stories and Storytellers**   105

Unit 9:   **Unusual Jobs**   117

Unit 10:   **Uncovering the Past**   131

Unit 11:   **Plastic Planet**   145

Unit 12:   **Vanished!**   159

Credits and Acknowledgments   173

Glossary / Exam Question Type Index   175

Tips for Effective Reading   176

SCOPE AND SEQUENCE

UNIT	THEME	READING	VIDEO
1	Amazing Animals	A: The Incredible Dolphin B: Master of Disguise	A Chameleon's Colors
2	Travel and Adventure	A: The Trip of a Lifetime B: Adventure Islands	Exploring Laponia
3	The Power of Music	A: Move to the Music B: A Musical Boost	The Mozart Effect
4	Into Space	A: Life Beyond Earth? B: Living in Space	The Red Planet
5	City Life	A: Global Cities B: A Taste of Two Cities	New York Skyscraper
6	Backyard Discoveries	A: In One Cubic Foot B: What's in Your Neighborhood?	BioBlitz
7	When Dinosaurs Ruled	A: The Truth about Dinosaurs B: Mystery of the Terrible Hand	Dinosaurs: A Brief History
8	Stories and Storytellers	A: The Brothers Grimm B: The Seven Ravens	Fairy-tale Castle
9	Unusual Jobs	A: Meet the Meteorite Hunter B: Smokejumpers	Snake Catchers
10	Uncovering the Past	A: The Army's True Colors B: Wonders of Egypt	City in the Clouds
11	Plastic Planet	A: The Problem with Plastic B: Five Tips for Using Less Plastic	Our Plastic World
12	Vanished!	A: Mystery on the Mountain B: The Missing Pilot	Earhart Mystery

ACADEMIC SKILLS

READING SKILL	VOCABULARY BUILDING	CRITICAL THINKING
A: Skimming for Gist **B:** Identifying Main Ideas in Paragraphs	**A:** Suffixes *-ance* and *-ence* **B:** Word forms of *survive*	**A:** Identifying Ideas **B:** Comparing; Reflecting
A: Understanding Maps **B:** Scanning for Key Details	**A:** Words acting as nouns and verbs **B:** Collocations with *original*	**A:** Interpreting Visual Information **B:** Reflecting
A: Identifying Supporting Details **B:** Identifying Supporting Reasons (1)	**A:** Collocations with *control* **B:** Suffix *-ion*	**A:** Reflecting **B:** Relating to Personal Experience; Evaluating Methods
A: Summarizing: Using a Concept Map **B:** Identifying Supporting Reasons (2)	**A:** Suffix *-ful* **B:** Collocations with *environment*	**A:** Speculating **B:** Reflecting; Ranking Tasks
A: Understanding Charts and Graphs **B:** Summarizing: Using a T-chart (1)	**A:** Prefix *inter-* **B:** Suffix *-ation*	**A:** Ranking Cities **B:** Relating; Evaluating Pros and Cons
A: Understanding Sequence (1)—Processes **B:** Understanding Sequence (2)—Instructions or Directions	**A:** Phrasal verbs with *break* **B:** Collocations with *take*	**A:** Applying Ideas **B:** Analyzing Information; Applying Ideas
A: Identifying Supporting Examples **B:** Finding Meaning (1)—Using Definitions	**A:** Suffixes *-er* and *-or* **B:** Collocations with *opinion*	**A:** Analyzing Theories **B:** Speculating; Reflecting
A: Annotating Text (1) **B:** Understanding Pronoun Reference	**A:** Suffix *-al* **B:** Word usage: *affect* vs. *effect*	**A:** Analyzing Stories **B:** Applying Ideas; Making Predictions
A: Identifying Exact vs. Approximate Numbers **B:** Annotating Text (2)	**A:** Collocations with *treasure* **B:** Suffix *-ment*	**A:** Justifying an Opinion **B:** Ranking/Speculating; Reflecting
A: Finding Meaning (2)—Identifying Homonyms **B:** Creating an Outline Summary	**A:** Collocations with *reveal* **B:** Collocations with *task*	**A:** Evaluating Pros and Cons **B:** Analyzing Evidence; Justifying an Opinion
A: Understanding a Writer's Use of Quotes **B:** Finding Meaning (3)—Using Context	**A:** Prefix *ex-* **B:** Collocations with *global*	**A:** Inferring Effects **B:** Ranking Suggestions; Applying Ideas
A: Summarizing: Using a T-chart (2) **B:** Recognizing Degrees of Certainty	**A:** Suffix *-ever* **B:** Prefix *dis-*	**A:** Evaluating Evidence **B:** Evaluating Theories; Reflecting

READING EXPLORER brings the world to your classroom.

With *Reading Explorer* you learn about real people and places, experience the world, and explore topics that matter.

What you'll see in the Third Edition:

Real-world stories give you a better understanding of the world and your place in it.

National Geographic Videos expand on the unit topic and give you a chance to apply your language skills.

Reading Skill and **Reading Comprehension** sections provide the tools you need to become an effective reader.

READING SKILL

Summarizing: Using a Concept Map

When you summarize a text, you record the main ideas and key details. A concept map can help you organize these ideas in a clear and logical way, and can help you understand information better. In a concept map, the main ideas are linked by words and phrases that explain the connection between them.

You can create a concept map by first starting with a main idea, topic, or issue. Then note the key concepts that link to this main idea. The bigger and more general concepts come first, which are then linked to smaller, more specific concepts.

ANALYZING   **A.** Look back at Reading A. Find the main ideas and key details in the text.

SUMMARIZING   **B.** Complete the concept map below with words or phrases from Reading A.

> unlikely only one planet in ¹_____ years has intelligent life

> using powerful ⁴_____, so we can now see solar systems that we could not before

SUMMARIZING   **B.** Complete the concept map with words or phrases from the reading.

Review this reading skill in Unit 4A

Asia
• Beijing and ¹_____ will be very powerful
• More business potential in other Chinese and ²_____ cities

FUTURE GLOBAL CITIES

South America
• Several cities will be more powerful due to the rise of the ³_____

Middle East
• Cities in Turkey, ⁴_____, and the UAE will have more power in world ⁵_____ and business

CRITICAL THINKING Evaluating Theories   Discuss these questions with a partner.

▶ Look back at Reading B. Of the theories about Amelia Earhart's disappearance, which does the author think is most likely?
Theory: _____

▶ Do you agree with the author? What do you think happened to Earhart and Noonan? Note your answers below. Then compare them with your ideas in Before You Read B (on page 166).
_____

Expanded Vocabulary Practice sections teach you the most useful words and phrases needed for academic reading.

WORD PARTS   **C.** The suffix *-ful* in **powerful** means "full of." Complete the sentences using the words in the box. One word is extra.

care	harm	power	wonder

1. Moon dust can be _____ful and can damage our DNA.
2. Astronomers need to be very _____ful with the expensive equipment they use.
3. The Falcon Heavy rocket is extremely _____ful. It can carry a load of 60,000 kg.

AMAZING ANIMALS

> **A great gray owl is camouflaged against a tree.**

WARM UP

Discuss these questions with a partner.

1. What is your favorite animal? Why?

2. What are some things animals can do that humans can't?

1A

BEFORE YOU READ

LABELING

A. Look at the photo. Match each description (1–4) with the correct part of the dolphin.

1. Dolphins sleep by resting one half of their **brain** at a time.

2. A dolphin's **tail** doesn't have any bones.

3. Dolphins "hear" through a special bone in their lower **jaw**.

4. The bones inside a dolphin's **flippers** look like the bones inside your arm and hand.

SKIMMING

B. Look at the reading title and headings. What is the reading about? Circle a, b, or c. Then read the passage to check your answer.

a. types of dolphins

b. things dolphins do

c. what dolphins eat

> A spotted dolphin swims in the clear waters of the Caribbean.

THE INCREDIBLE DOLPHIN

A Many people say dolphins are **intelligent**. They seem to be able to think, understand, and learn things quickly. But are they as **smart** as humans, or are they more like cats and dogs? Dolphins use their brains quite differently from the way people do. But scientists say dolphins and humans are **alike** in some ways. How?

Communication

B Like humans, every dolphin has its own "name." The name is a **special** whistle.[1] Each dolphin chooses a whistle for itself, usually by its first birthday. Dolphins are like people in other ways, too. They "talk" to each other about a lot of things—such as their age, their feelings, and possible danger. They also use a **system** of sounds and body language to **communicate**. Understanding dolphin conversation is not easy for humans. No one "speaks dolphin" yet, but some scientists are trying to learn.

Play

C Dolphins live in groups called *pods*, and they often join other dolphins from different pods to play games and have fun—just like people. Sometimes they chase other dolphins carrying objects (e.g., seaweed) and throw these objects back and forth. Scientists believe playing together is something only intelligent animals do.

Teamwork

D Dolphins and humans are similar in another way: They both make plans for getting things they want. In the seas of southern Brazil, for example, dolphins use an intelligent **method** to get food. When there are fish near a boat, dolphins signal[2] to the fishermen to put their nets in the water. With the dolphins' help, the men can catch a lot of fish. Why do dolphins **assist** the men? There is an **advantage** for the dolphins: They get to eat some of the fish that escape from the net.

---

1 A **whistle** is a high-pitched sound made by blowing air through a hole.
2 If you **signal** to someone, you make an action or a sound to tell them something.

READING COMPREHENSION

A. Choose the best answer for each question.

MAIN IDEA

1. What does the reading NOT mention?

    a. how dolphins communicate with each other

    b. how dolphins move quickly through the water

    c. how dolphins play games and have fun

INFERENCE

2. The author mentions cats and dogs in paragraph A to show that _____.

    a. cats and dogs are very intelligent

    b. there are different levels of intelligence

    c. scientists have studied the brains of cats and dogs

DETAIL

3. Where does a dolphin get its "name"?

    a. It gets it from its mother.

    b. It gets it from scientists.

    c. It chooses it for itself.

DETAIL

4. Which sentence about dolphin language is true?

    a. Dolphins "talk" to each other about many things.

    b. Dolphin conversation is easy for humans to understand.

    c. Dolphins can't understand dolphins from other pods.

DETAIL

5. Why do dolphins sometimes help fishermen?

    a. Dolphins are kind animals.

    b. The dolphins can get food that way.

    c. The fishermen ask the dolphins for help.

CATEGORIZING

B. According to the reading passage, what do these dolphin behaviors (a–f) demonstrate? Add them to the chart.

    a. using body language
    d. joining other pods for games

    b. chasing each other
    e. helping fishermen catch fish

    c. whistling
    f. throwing seaweed back and forth

Communication	Play	Teamwork

A bottlenose dolphin in the
Bay of Islands, New Zealand

Skimming for Gist

The **gist** of a passage is what the text is mainly about. When you want to get the gist of a passage, don't read every word. Skim the text quickly to find out what it is mostly about. Look at the title and any headings, photos, and captions. Another strategy is to read the first sentence of each paragraph.

SKIMMING

A. Skim Reading A again. What is the main idea of the passage? Circle a, b, or c.

   a. We can learn a lot from the way dolphins communicate, play, and work together.
   b. The dolphin is the most intelligent sea animal in the world.
   c. Dolphins are intelligent and—in some ways—are like humans.

SKIMMING

B. Skim this short passage and answer the questions (1–2) below. Then read the passage again and check your answers.

The albatross is one of the world's largest flying birds. It also has the largest wings of any bird—up to 3.4 meters from tip to tip. These giant birds use their wings to ride the ocean winds. They can fly for hours without rest, or even without moving their wings. Some may even be able to sleep while flying.

Most albatrosses spend nearly all their time in the air. In fact, they only return to land to breed.[1] A parent albatross might fly thousands of kilometers to find food for its young. In its lifetime, an albatross can fly a total of more than six million kilometers.

⌄ A wandering albatross

----

1 When animals **breed**, they have babies.

1. What is the above passage mainly about?

   a. where albatrosses live
   b. albatross flying behavior
   c. albatross intelligence

2. What could be a title for this passage?

   a. Riding the Ocean Winds
   b. Catching Fish
   c. The Smartest Bird

CRITICAL THINKING Identifying Ideas

▶ Reading A mentions three similarities between dolphins and humans. What are they?

_____   _____   _____

▶ Can you think of other ways to tell if an animal is intelligent? Discuss with a partner and note some ideas.

_____

_____

DEFINITIONS **A.** Read the paragraph below and match each word in **red** with its definition (1–5).

There are a few ways to test how **smart** animals are. One **method** is to test memory. Scientists in Japan showed a group of college students and a group of five-year-old chimps the numbers 1 to 9 in different places on a computer screen. The test was to see if the groups could remember the position of the numbers in the correct order. Each time, the chimps were faster than the students. Why? Were the chimps **special** in some way? Did someone **assist** them? No, but the chimps probably had an important **advantage**: They were young. As both humans and animals get older, their memory gets worse.

1. _____ : a way of doing something

2. _____ : to help

3. _____ : clever

4. _____ : better or more important than others

5. _____ : something that helps you succeed

COMPLETION **B.** Complete the information with the words from the box.

| alike   communicate   feelings   intelligent   system |

Orangutans and humans are ¹_____
in some ways. Both are very ²_____
animals. For example, to stay dry when it rains,
orangutans take leaves from trees and use them
like umbrellas. These apes don't have a complex[1]
language ³_____ like humans do. But
today, some orangutans are learning basic sign
language to express their thoughts and ⁴_____ .
New research also suggests that orangutans can
⁵_____ about the past, just like humans.

> A Sumatran orangutan

1 If something is **complex**, it is complicated or made up of many parts.

WORD PARTS **C.** Some nouns use the suffixes *-ance* and *-ence*. Use the noun form of these words to complete the sentences. Add the correct suffix to each word.

| assist   different   intelligent |

1. What is the _____ between a dolphin and a porpoise?

2. The fact that apes use tools shows they have great _____ .

3. Whales will often give _____ to other whales that are in danger.

BEFORE YOU READ

DEFINITIONS **A.** Read the caption below. Then circle the correct words to complete these definitions.

1. If you **disguise** yourself, you change how you look so others *know* / *don't know* who you are.

2. A **predator** is an animal that eats *other animals* / *plants*.

3. If two animals **look like** each other, they look *different* / *the same*.

SKIMMING **B.** Look at the picture on page 15 and read the caption and labels. Then skim the passage and complete the sentence below. Read the passage to check your answer.

Review this reading skill in Unit 1A

Most of the passage explains *why* / *how* octopuses disguise themselves.

Octopuses **disguise** themselves so **predators** (e.g., dolphins or sharks) don't see them. Here, the octopus **looks like** the coral nearby.

MASTER OF DISGUISE

A Octopuses are famous for their round bodies, big eyes, and eight arms. There are many different types of octopuses, but all are alike in one way: They are masters[1] of disguise. Octopuses can change their **appearance** in less than a second to look like rocks, plants, or even other animals. How do they do this?

B An octopus can disguise itself in three ways. One is by using color. An octopus's skin has special cells[2] called *chromatophores*. These cells are filled with yellow, brown, and red pigment.[3] When an octopus moves its **muscles** a certain way, the cells become large and **produce** colorful spots and other **patterns** on its skin. Chromatophores can also reflect light. In blue light, for example, an octopus's skin will look blue. In white light, its skin will look white. With these cells, an octopus can produce many different skin colors and patterns.

C An octopus can also change its skin texture.[4] When the octopus moves its muscles, its skin can go from smooth to spiky. It might then look like a plant, or coral. Another way an octopus disguises itself is by changing its **shape**. Some, for example, roll their bodies into balls so they look like rocks. One type of octopus can change its form to look like other sea **creatures**—especially dangerous ones, such as sea snakes.

D Why are octopuses so good at disguising themselves? They have to be. The ocean is not a safe place for them. Because they have no bones in their bodies, octopuses are like large pieces of meat. Many predators want to eat them—and they can eat them whole. To **survive**, octopuses have **developed** the amazing **ability** to change their appearance very quickly in order to **hide** from predators.

---

1 A **master** is very good at doing something.
2 A **cell** is the smallest living part of an animal or plant. Most animals have billions of cells in their bodies.
3 **Pigment** is a substance that gives something color. For example, green pigment makes most plants look green.
4 **Texture** is how something looks and feels (e.g., soft, smooth, spiky).

ALL MUSCLE, NO BONES

An octopus's body has many muscles. This makes it strong and fast. Octopuses also have no bones, so they can change their shape very quickly.

An octopus brain holds only one-third of the animal's neurons (nerve cells). It handles functions such as decision-making, learning, and memory.

An octopus has three hearts: one large central heart and two smaller ones on either side.

About two-thirds of an octopus's neurons are in its arms. These neurons control the arm movements.

Octopuses can change their appearance to match their surroundings. Once the brain gives a signal, the octopus's muscles move in a certain way, changing its skin from smooth to spiky and producing colorful spots or stripes on its skin.

Skin texture	Skin color/pattern
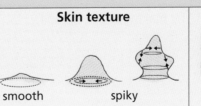	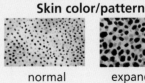
smooth spiky	normal expanded (large spots)

A. Choose the best answer for each question.

GIST
1. What would be the best alternative title for this passage?

    a. The Mind of an Octopus

    b. How an Octopus Hides

    c. Octopus Numbers on the Rise

DETAIL
2. Which of these sentences is NOT true?

    a. Chromatophores are light-reflecting cells.

    b. Chromatophores can change in size.

    c. Chromatophores produce an animal's skin texture.

INFERENCE
3. In red light, an octopus probably appears _____ .

    a. red

    b. blue

    c. white

INFERENCE
4. In paragraph C, the author suggests that some corals _____ .

    a. can change their color

    b. can roll themselves into balls

    c. have spiky outer surfaces

REFERENCE
5. What does *they* refer to in paragraph D, line 4?

    a. octopuses

    b. bones

    c. predators

MATCHING
B. Look at the list of ways octopuses disguise themselves (a–c) and the statements (1–5). Match each statement with the method of disguise. Write a, b, or c.

a. color   b. skin texture   c. shape

_____ **1.** by producing spots on their skin

_____ **2.** by appearing to be sea snakes

_____ **3.** by rolling their bodies into balls

_____ **4.** by reflecting light

_____ **5.** by making their skin spiky

> **A Pacific red octopus shows its suckers.**

Identifying Main Ideas in Paragraphs

A paragraph usually has one main idea and some details that support it. Paragraphs often include a topic sentence that describes the main idea. Usually—but not always—a topic sentence is at or near the start of the paragraph, or at the end. One way to find the main idea quickly is to read the sentences at the beginning and end of the paragraph. A paragraph's heading (if it has one) can also give a clue to its main idea.

MAIN IDEA

A. Read the paragraph below. Which sentence gives the main idea? Circle a, b, or c.

Is it a stick? Or is it an insect? It's a stick insect— an insect that looks like a stick. The stick insect is an example of an animal that uses color, texture, and shape to disguise itself. It lives— and can easily hide—among the leaves and twigs of plants. Most stick insects are either brown or green. The smallest types are just over a centimeter long. The largest is about 33 centimeters, making it one of the world's longest insects.

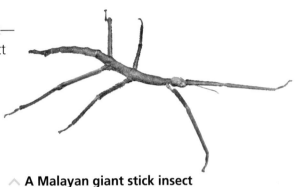

△ **A Malayan giant stick insect**

a. The stick insect is an example of an animal that uses color, texture, and shape to disguise itself.

b. It lives—and can easily hide—among the leaves and twigs of plants.

c. The largest is about 33 centimeters, making it one of the world's longest insects.

MAIN IDEA

B. Look back at Reading B. Match each paragraph with its main idea (a–d).

1. Paragraph A •

2. Paragraph B •

3. Paragraph C •

4. Paragraph D •

• a. An octopus can change its shape and skin texture.

• b. Octopuses can change how they look very quickly.

• c. An octopus can change its skin color.

• d. Octopuses disguise themselves for their own protection.

CRITICAL THINKING Comparing   Which animal do you think is smarter—the dolphin or the octopus? Why? Note your ideas and discuss with a partner.

COMPLETION   **A.** Complete the paragraph with words from the box.

ability	appearance	hide	patterns	produce

Reef squid—like their relatives, octopuses—have an amazing
¹_____ : They can quickly change their physical
²_____ in order to ³_____ from
predators. They also use this skill to send messages; they can
even ⁴_____ two messages at the same time!
For example, a male reef squid swimming near a female squid
can create colorful, attractive ⁵_____ on the side
of its body closest to the female. On the other side, it shows
black and white lines that tell other male squid to stay away.

▽ **A bigfin reef squid**

WORDS IN CONTEXT   **B.** Complete each sentence with the correct answer (a or b).

1. A **creature** refers to any living _____.
   a. plant
   b. animal

2. A circle has a _____ **shape**.
   a. round
   b. square

3. If you **survive** a dangerous situation, you _____ through it.
   a. live
   b. don't live

4. The **muscles** in the human body control how we _____.
   a. think
   b. move

5. If you **develop** a skill or ability, it becomes _____.
   a. better or stronger
   b. worse or weaker

WORD FORMS   **C.** The verb **survive** can be made into a noun by adding the suffixes *-or* or *-al*. Complete the sentences with the correct words from the box.

survive	survivor	survival

1. The _____ of whales is connected to the health of the ocean.

2. These plants cannot _____ in very cold conditions.

3. The plane crash had only one _____.

> A chameleon balances on a thin branch.

A CHAMELEON'S COLORS

BEFORE YOU WATCH

PREVIEWING **A.** Read the extracts from the video. Then complete the definitions of the words or phrases in **bold**. Circle the correct words.

"Chameleons can change color to **attract** other chameleons or to **warn** them to go away."

"To catch food, a chameleon hides in the trees until an insect walks by. Then it **shoots out** its tongue …"

1. If you want to **attract** something, you want it to *come to you / go away*.

2. When you **warn** someone about something, you tell them that something *good / bad* may happen.

3. When something **shoots out**, it moves very *quickly / slowly*.

QUIZ **B.** Read the sentences below and guess if they are correct. Circle **T** (true) or **F** (false).

1. The main reason chameleons change color is to hide from predators.   **T**   **F**

2. A chameleon's tongue is very long.   **T**   **F**

3. Chameleons are in trouble because they are being hunted by other animals.   **T**   **F**

WHILE YOU WATCH

GIST   **A.** Watch the video. Check your answers in Before You Watch B.

MULTIPLE CHOICE   **B.** Watch the video again. Choose the correct answer for each question.

1. According to the video, where do many different types of chameleons live?

    a. Malta

    b. Madagascar

2. What is one reason given in the video for chameleons' color changes?

    a. to show that they want some food

    b. to show that they are scared

3. Why do chameleons rock back and forth?

    a. to stay safe from predators

    b. to get ready to attack other animals

4. The video uses a model of a bow and arrow to _____ .

    a. show how difficult it is for a predator to attack a chameleon

    b. explain how a chameleon can stick out its tongue very fast

CRITICAL THINKING Reflecting   If you were a scientist studying animals, what animal would you study? What would you like to find out about this animal? Note some ideas and share your answers with a partner.

_____

_____

_____

VOCABULARY REVIEW

Do you remember the meanings of these words? Check (✓) the ones you know. Look back at the unit and review any words you're not sure of.

Reading A

☐ advantage ☐ alike ☐ assist* ☐ communicate* ☐ feelings

☐ intelligent* ☐ method* ☐ smart ☐ special ☐ system

Reading B

☐ ability ☐ appearance ☐ creature ☐ develop ☐ hide

☐ muscle ☐ pattern ☐ produce ☐ shape ☐ survive*

* Academic Word List

TRAVEL AND ADVENTURE

Hikers on the Charles
Kuonen Suspension Bridge
in Randa, Switzerland

WARM UP

Discuss these questions with a partner.

1. Which places in the world would you
   most like to visit? Why?

2. What is the most adventurous trip
   you have been on?

CYCLING THE AMERICAS

In 2005, Gregg Bleakney and his friend Brooks Allen began an amazing two-year cycling adventure.

Route ⟿

Total distance: 30,500 kilometers

▦ mountains

START
Prudhoe Bay, AK ⊙

● San Francisco, CA

● Mexico City, Mexico

Panama City, Panama

La Paz, Bolivia

FINISH ⊙ Ushuaia, Argentina

BEFORE YOU READ

SCANNING **A.** Use the map and the information above to answer these questions.

1. Where did the two friends travel from and to? How did they travel?

2. How far did they travel? How long did the trip take?

DISCUSSION **B.** Why do you think they wanted to make this trip? Discuss with a partner.

THE TRIP OF A LIFETIME

A   Many people dream of going on a great travel adventure. Most of us keep dreaming; others make it happen.

B   Gregg Bleakney's dream was to travel the Americas from top to bottom. He got the idea after he finished a 1,600-kilometer bike ride. Gregg's friend Brooks Allen was also a cyclist. The two friends talked and decided on their **goal**: They would travel from Alaska to Argentina—by bike.

C   To pay for the **journey**, Gregg and Brooks worked and saved money for years. In 2005, after four years of planning, they set off. Once they were on the road, they often camped outdoors or stayed in hostels.[1] In many places along their **route**, local people opened their homes to the two friends and gave them food.

---

1   A **hostel** is a cheap place to stay when traveling.

In Guatemala, Brooks Allen and Gregg Bleakney cycled through Tikal National Park.

Lessons from the Road

D During their trip, Gregg and Brooks cycled through deserts, rain forests, and mountains. They visited **modern** cities and explored **ancient** ruins,[2] such as Tikal in Guatemala. In many places, they met other cyclists from all over the world.

E In May 2007—two years, 12 countries, and over 30,500 km later—Gregg eventually reached Ushuaia, Argentina, at the southern tip of South America. (Halfway through the trip, Brooks had to stop. He returned to the United States and Gregg continued without him.)

F Gregg and Brooks kept a **record** of their adventures in an online blog. The trip taught both men a lot about traveling. Here is some of Gregg's **advice**.

- **Travel light.** The less baggage you have, the less you'll **worry** about.
- **Be flexible.** Don't plan everything. You'll be more **relaxed** and happy, even when there are **challenges** along the way.
- **Be polite.** As one traveler told Gregg, "Always remember that nobody wants to fight, cheat, or rob[3] a nice guy."

---

2 The **ruins** of something are the parts that remain after it is damaged or weakened.
3 If someone **robs** you, they take money or property from you.

∨ **Many Antarctic cruises start from the port of Ushuaia in Argentina.**

A. Choose the best answer for each question.

GIST
1. What could be another title for the reading?

a. Cycling from Alaska to Argentina
b. Things to Do and See in America
c. Argentina: The Land of Adventure

DETAIL
2. Which sentence about the trip is NOT true?

a. To pay for the trip, Gregg and Brooks saved money and traveled cheaply on the road.
b. During their trip, Gregg and Brooks met cyclists from all around the world.
c. Only Brooks made the complete trip from Alaska to Argentina.

VOCABULARY
3. In paragraph F, what does *baggage* mean?

a. things you take on a trip
b. places you visit on a trip
c. reasons for going on a trip

PARAPHRASE
4. What does Gregg mean by *Be flexible* in paragraph F?

a. Be careful when you travel.
b. Be ready to change easily.
c. Plan the details of your trip.

⌃ **In Prudhoe Bay, Alaska, the sun does not set from mid-May through mid-July.**

INFERENCE
5. Which statement would Gregg most likely agree with?

a. When you travel, only stay in hotels or with people you know.
b. Bring a lot of things on your trip so you don't have to buy anything.
c. When abroad, learn how to say "thank you" in the local language.

MAIN IDEA **B.** Match each paragraph with its main idea.

Review this reading skill in Unit 1B

1. Paragraph B •
• a. what the cyclists saw on their trip

2. Paragraph C •
• b. what the cyclists learned from their trip

3. Paragraph D •
• c. a dream of cycling through the Americas

4. Paragraph E •
• d. how the cyclists paid for their trip

5. Paragraph F •
• e. when and where the cycling trip ended

Understanding Maps

Like other visuals, maps can help you better understand a text. Most maps have a **title**, a **scale** (to show distance), a **key** or **legend** (a guide of symbols or colors used), and a **source** (where the information comes from). A map may also include a **compass** (to show where north is).

LABELING   **A.** Look at the map below. Label the parts of the map with these features (1–5).

1. key   **2.** source   **3.** scale   **4.** title   **5.** compass

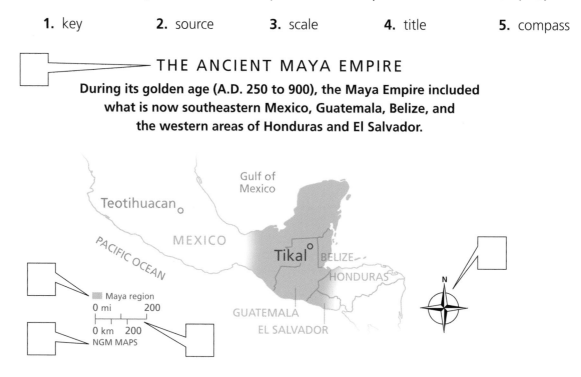

THE ANCIENT MAYA EMPIRE

During its golden age (A.D. 250 to 900), the Maya Empire included what is now southeastern Mexico, Guatemala, Belize, and the western areas of Honduras and El Salvador.

COMPLETION   **B.** Use information from the map above to complete these sentences. Circle the correct words.

1. The ancient city of Teotihuacan in Mexico *was / was not* part of the Maya Empire.

2. The distance from Teotihuacan to Tikal is *less / greater* than 400 kilometers.

3. Tikal is located in *northern / southern* Guatemala. It is close to the border with *Honduras / Belize*.

CRITICAL THINKING Interpreting Visual Information   Look back at the map on page 22. Which parts of the journey do you think were the most challenging for the cyclists? Why? Discuss with a partner and note your ideas.

_____

_____

VOCABULARY PRACTICE

WORDS IN CONTEXT

A. Complete each sentence with the correct answer (a or b).

1. If something is **ancient**, it is very _____ .

   a. expensive   b. old

2. _____ is an example of a **modern** invention.

   a. The cell phone   b. Paper

3. A **record** of an event will help you _____ it.

   a. change   b. remember

4. If something is a **challenge**, it is _____ to do.

   a. difficult   b. easy

COMPLETION

B. Complete the information using words from the box.

> **advice goals journey relax route worry**

Every year, many people make mistakes when they go hiking.

Here's some ¹_____ that can help you stay safe.

Before you start your ²_____, leave a map showing the

³_____ that you are planning to take. If something goes

wrong (for example, if you get lost), you should "S.T.O.P." This means:

- **S**top: try to ⁴_____ and stay calm.
- **T**hink about your situation.
- **O**bserve: look around and notice where you are.
- **P**lan what to do next: set one or two simple
  ⁵_____ for yourself.

It's also important to stay on clearly marked trails. Don't

⁶_____—someone will eventually find you.

⌄ **Hikers in the Austrian Tyrol**

WORD USAGE

C. Some words such as **record** can be either a noun (pronounced "**re**cord") or a verb (pronounced "re**cord**"). Complete the sentences with the correct words from the box. Then circle the stressed syllable in each word.

> **address   object   record**

1. We found a strange _____ among the ruins.

2. Once I've found somewhere to live, I'll send you my new _____.

3. You should _____ your travels in a travel diary.

Land diving on Pentecost Island, Vanuatu

BEFORE YOU READ

DISCUSSION   **A.**   Look at the photo. Then answer the questions below with a partner.

     1. What do you think is happening in the photo?

     2. What is the most dangerous sport or activity you have tried?

PREDICTING   **B.**   Look at the reading title and headings. What do you think these activities have in common? Check your ideas as you read.

ADVENTURE ISLANDS

A Vanuatu is a **nation** of small islands in the South Pacific. It is one of the smallest countries in the world. But for those interested in adventure and sport, there is a lot to do. Some of the best swimming, snorkeling, and sea kayaking can be found here. Vanuatu's islands also offer visitors two of the most exciting—and dangerous—activities in the world: volcano surfing and land diving.

Volcano Surfing

B On Tanna Island, Mount Yasur rises 300 meters into the sky. Yasur is one of Vanuatu's few **active** volcanoes. It erupts[1] **almost** every day, sometimes several times a day. For **centuries**, both locals and tourists have climbed this mountain to visit the top. Recently, people have also started climbing Yasur to surf the volcano. In some ways, volcano surfing is like surfing in the sea, but in other ways, it's very different. A volcano surfer's goal is to **escape** the erupting volcano—without being **hit** by flying rocks! It's fast, fun, and dangerous—the perfect extreme sport.[2]

Land Diving

C Most people are **familiar** with bungee jumping. But did you know that bungee jumping started on Pentecost Island in Vanuatu almost 15 centuries ago? The **original** activity—called land diving—is part of a religious ceremony.[3] A man **ties** two tree vines[4] around his ankles. He then climbs a wooden tower around 20 to 30 meters high, crosses his arms, and jumps headfirst. The goal is to touch the earth with the top of his head—without breaking the vines or hitting the ground hard. Every spring, local boys and men still perform this amazing test of **bravery**. Women are not allowed to dive, but they support the divers by dancing and singing at the bottom of the tower. Many tourists come to the island every year to watch this ancient tradition.

---

1 When a volcano **erupts**, it throws out hot rock called lava.

2 An **extreme sport** is a sport that is dangerous and exciting, such as skydiving or bungee jumping.

3 A **ceremony** is a formal event, such as a wedding.

4 A **vine** is a plant that grows up or over things.

A. Choose the best answer for each question.

PURPOSE
1. What is the purpose of this reading?

    a. to compare Vanuatu with other islands in the South Pacific
    b. to explain what volcano surfing and land diving are
    c. to talk about the world's best volcano surfer and land diver

MAIN IDEA
2. How are volcano surfing and land diving similar?

    a. They are both ancient sports.
    b. Anyone can do them.
    c. They are both extreme activities.

REFERENCE
3. In paragraph A, what does *those* refer to?

    a. people
    b. countries
    c. islands

DETAIL
4. Which sentence is true about Mount Yasur?

    a. It is no longer active.
    b. People have been climbing it for a long time.
    c. It is on Pentecost Island.

> ∧ **Vanuatu is also a popular destination for scuba divers. Underwater creatures there include extremely colorful sea slugs like this one.**

DETAIL
5. Which sentence is true about land diving?

    a. It was first called "bungee jumping."
    b. It is less popular today than in the past.
    c. It is a traditional activity in Vanuatu.

EVALUATING STATEMENTS
B. Are the following statements true or false according to the reading passage, or is the information not given? Circle **T** (true), **F** (false), or **NG** (not given).

1. Vanuatu has more than one active volcano.	**T**	**F**	**NG**
2. Volcano surfing came to Vanuatu from another country.	**T**	**F**	**NG**
3. More people get hurt volcano surfing than land diving.	**T**	**F**	**NG**
4. Both men and women can do land diving.	**T**	**F**	**NG**
5. The land diving ceremony is a popular tourist attraction.	**T**	**F**	**NG**

Scanning for Key Details

When you read, you often want to find specific details in the text. Before you read, you first need to decide what to look for (e.g., a person's name, a place, or a number). Once you know what to look for, scan the text quickly to find that information.

ANALYZING **A.** Read the questions. What kind of answer will you need to scan for? Circle a, b, or c. (Do not answer the questions yet.)

1. Where can you surf in cold water?

    a. a place   b. a number   c. a date

2. How high are the highest waves on the "silver dragon"?

    a. an example   b. a number   c. a reason

3. Why is surfing possible in so many places?

    a. a reason   b. a place   c. an example

4. What other hobby is popular among surfers?

    a. a place   b. a reason   c. an activity

SCANNING **B.** Now scan the text below and write answers to the questions above.

1. _____

2. _____

3. _____

4. _____

When you think of surfing, you probably think of Hawaii, Australia, or Brazil. But surfers don't need warm weather, or even an ocean. For example, some surfers ride the waves in the icy cold waters of Antarctica. Other surfers head to China's Qiantang River to surf the "silver dragon." Twice a year, the waves on the Qiantang can reach a height of 10 meters.

Surfing is possible in all these places because a surfer only needs two things: a wave and a board. There is always a risk, so surfers need to be strong swimmers. They also need good balance and an ability to think and move quickly. This is why skateboarding is a common hobby among surfers.

CRITICAL THINKING Reflecting   Imagine a tourist wants to try an extreme sport or activity in your country. Where would you suggest they go? What should they do? Note some ideas and share them with a partner.

_____

_____

COMPLETION **A.** Circle the correct words to complete the information below.

If you lead an [1]**almost / active** lifestyle and want to learn an extreme water sport, consider whitewater kayaking. Many people head to Chile every year to kayak along the many rivers and rapids[1] that the [2]**bravery / nation** is known for. The United States also has many popular kayaking spots, such as the Great Falls of the Potomac River. The falls lie [3]**almost / familiar** entirely within the state of Maryland.

Whitewater kayaking is very dangerous. So why do people do it? For some, it is a test of [4]**centuries / bravery**. For others, it makes them feel alive.

1 **Rapids** are a section of a river where the water moves very fast, often over rocks.

▲ **A whitewater kayaker on the Potomac River**

DEFINITIONS **B.** Complete the definitions using words from the box. One word is extra.

active   century   escape   familiar   hit   original   tie

1. If you _____ something, you touch it with a lot of force.

2. Something that is _____ is the very first of its kind.

3. A(n) _____ is a period of a hundred years.

4. If you are _____ with something, you know or understand it well.

5. If you _____ two things together, you join them using rope or string.

6. If you _____ from something, you run away from it.

COLLOCATIONS **C.** The nouns in the box are often used with the word **original**. Complete the sentences with the correct nouns from the box.

idea   owner   song

1. The land was returned to its original _____ .

2. The students came up with a very original _____ for how to solve the problem.

3. We wrote and performed an original _____ for the music competition.

A view of the Northern Lights over Laponia, Sweden (photographed by Orsolya Haarberg)

EXPLORING LAPONIA

BEFORE YOU WATCH

PREVIEWING

A. Read the information. The words in **bold** appear in the video. Circle the correct words to complete the definitions (1–3).

Laponia (in Sweden) is a large **wilderness** area of high mountains, ancient forests, and beautiful lakes and rivers. A UNESCO World Heritage Site, it covers over 9,400 square kilometers of **untouched** nature. Erlend and Orsolya Haarberg—a husband-and-wife team of nature photographers—have made several trips to this area. On each trip, they carry a lot of food, clothes, cameras, and camping **gear**. Orsolya describes taking photos here as "a real adventure."

1. A **wilderness** is an area of natural land that *is / is not* used by people.

2. An **untouched** piece of land is *in its original state / cleaned by people*.

3. A photographer's **gear** is the *goal of their trip / set of things they take with them*.

PREDICTING

B. What kinds of challenges do you think the Haarbergs face on their trips to Laponia? Discuss with a partner and note some ideas.

_____

_____

GIST **A.** Watch the video. Were any of your predictions in Before You Watch B mentioned in the video? What other challenges are mentioned? Note them below.

_____

_____

SHORT ANSWER **B.** Watch the video again. Write a short answer for each question.

1. Is it easier to explore Laponia in winter or in summer? Why?

_____

2. What are some types of food the Haarbergs carry with them?

_____

3. What happened to Orsolya on one trip?

_____

CRITICAL THINKING Reflecting   Think about the activities or adventures you have learned about in this unit. Which ones would you want to try? Which ones would you not want to try? Note your answers and reasons, and share them with a partner.

_____

_____

_____

VOCABULARY REVIEW

Do you remember the meanings of these words? Check (✓) the ones you know. Look back at the unit and review any words you're not sure of.

Reading A

☐ advice ☐ ancient ☐ challenge* ☐ goal* ☐ journey

☐ modern ☐ record ☐ relaxed* ☐ route* ☐ worry

Reading B

☐ active ☐ almost ☐ bravery ☐ century ☐ escape

☐ familiar ☐ hit ☐ nation ☐ original ☐ tie

* Academic Word List

THE POWER OF MUSIC

Hip-hop group Migos performs at the 2018 Coachella Valley Music and Arts Festival in California.

WARM UP

Discuss these questions with a partner.

1. What is your favorite kind of music? Who is your favorite singer or band?

2. How important is music in your life? Give reasons and examples to support your answer.

BEFORE YOU READ

DISCUSSION **A.** Answer these questions with a partner.

1. How often do you exercise? What kind of exercise do you mostly do (e.g., go for a run, lift weights at the gym)?

2. When you exercise, do you listen to music? If so, what kind?

PREDICTING **B.** Read the caption above and discuss the question with a partner. Then read the passage to check your ideas.

A jogger passes the Petronas Twin Towers in Kuala Lumpur, Malaysia. Research shows that music helps us exercise—but why is this true?

MOVE
TO THE MUSIC

A Music helps us exercise—but why does it have this effect? Experts say there are two main reasons. The first is simple: Music **distracts** us. When we listen to a song we like, our brain **pays attention** to the music. For example, after we exercise for 20 minutes, our body might be tired. But we may not feel this immediately because we are listening to music. So we exercise a little longer.

B Music also motivates[1] us. When we hear dance music, for example, we naturally start to move to the **beat**. An upbeat[2] song also puts us in a good **mood**, so we feel happier. This gives us **energy** and helps us exercise longer. Music with a quick and **steady** beat is good for exercising. But the music shouldn't be *too* fast, says sports psychologist Dr. Costas Karageorghis. Generally, songs in the **range** of 120–140 beats per minute (BPM) are the best.

---

1 If something **motivates** you, it makes you want to do something.
2 An **upbeat** song is one that is lively and cheerful.

Beats per minute (BPM) is a term for measuring the speed of a piece of music. The higher the BPM, the faster the song. Here's a short playlist of popular workout music with the BPM for each song.

- "Lose Yourself" – Eminem (86 BPM)
- "Stronger (What Doesn't Kill You)" – Kelly Clarkson (116 BPM)
- "Idol" – BTS (126 BPM)
- "I Gotta Feeling" – The Black Eyed Peas (128 BPM)
- "On the Floor" – Jennifer Lopez featuring Pitbull (130 BPM)
- "Locked Out of Heaven" – Bruno Mars (144 BPM)
- "Mr. Brightside" – The Killers (148 BPM)

▲ **Bruno Mars is a Grammy Award-winning singer, songwriter, and producer.**

C A new study by cognitive scientist[3] Tom Fritz suggests this is only part of the explanation, however. In an experiment, Fritz put 61 people in small groups. They all then exercised twice. One time, each group worked out while listening to music for six minutes. Another time, they exercised for six minutes on special Jymmin machines. The name Jymmin is a combination of "jammin'" and "gym." Using these machines, each group made music as they moved. At the end, 53 of the 61 people said the same thing: They felt less tired when they exercised on the Jymmin machines. When we exercise and *make* music—especially with other people—working out **seems** to be easier.

D How does Fritz explain this? Maybe people did better on the Jymmin machines because they had more **control**, he says. People created the beat. They could make it go faster or slower. Also, the activity was **social**. Each group was making music together and having fun. Fritz believes that Jymmin exercise may have other advantages, too. He wants to find out if it can help with more serious conditions. For example, it may even be a good way to treat depression.[4]

---

3 A **cognitive scientist** is a person who studies the mind and how people think and learn.
4 **Depression** is a medical condition in which a person feels very sad and is often unable to live in a normal way.

A group of people exercise using Jymmin machines.

A. Choose the best answer for each question.

GIST

1. What is the reading mainly about?

    a. the effect of music on exercise

    b. good songs for a workout music playlist

    c. how Jymmin machines work

VOCABULARY

2. In paragraph A, what does the word *immediately* mean?

    a. completely

    b. sometimes

    c. right away

DETAIL

3. According to the passage, which of these songs is at the ideal speed for exercising?

    a. "Lose Yourself" – Eminem

    b. "I Gotta Feeling" – The Black Eyed Peas

    c. "Locked Out of Heaven" – Bruno Mars

MAIN IDEA

4. Paragraphs C and D focus on the advantages of _____ while exercising.

    a. listening to music

    b. watching music videos

    c. creating music

INFERENCE

5. Which of these can we definitely say about Jymmin machines?

    a. People exercised better using the machines because they had more control.

    b. People using the machines could make the music go faster or slower.

    c. The machines are useful in treating depression.

SUMMARIZING

B. Complete the summary below using words from the box. One word is extra.

control	**depression**	**distracts**	**make**	**motivate**	**range**	**tired**

One reason listening to music helps us exercise is that it ¹_____ us.

When we listen to a song we enjoy, our mind pays attention to the music, so we don't

feel ²_____. Another reason music helps us exercise is that it can

³_____ us to keep exercising.

A recent study shows that people exercise better when they use special machines

that allow them to ⁴_____ music while exercising with other people.

They felt this gave them more ⁵_____. Also, it made exercising a fun,

social activity. In the future, these machines could even be used to help people who

suffer from ⁶_____.

Identifying Supporting Details

The main ideas of a text are usually supported by details. These give more information about the main idea, and can include examples, facts, or reasons.

MATCHING

A. The sentences below (1–3) relate to Reading A. Match each sentence with the type of supporting detail it contains (a, b, or c).

a. example   b. fact   c. reason

_____ **1.** Dr. Tom Fritz works at the Max Planck Institute for Human Cognitive and Brain Sciences.

_____ **2.** Jymmin exercise may help even serious conditions such as depression.

_____ **3.** Music helps us exercise because it distracts us.

SUPPORTING DETAILS

B. Read this paragraph and underline the main idea. Then use supporting details in the paragraph to answer the questions (1–3).

Generally, songs with 120–140 beats per minute (BPM) are the best for exercising. This is because most people want to get their heart rate up to this level during a workout. Songs in this range include Lady Gaga's "The Edge of Glory" (128 BPM) and "Push It" (130 BPM) by Salt-N-Pepa. Listening to songs like these can increase your endurance[1] by up to 15 percent. A slower song like Adele's "Make You Feel My Love" (72 BPM) is more likely to make you want to relax, or even take a nap.

1 **Endurance** is the ability to keep doing something difficult, unpleasant, or painful for a long time.

1. Why are songs in the 120–140 BPM range good for exercising?

_____

2. Who sang the song "The Edge of Glory"?

_____

⌃ **In 2015, Adele's *25* broke the iTunes record for fastest-selling album.**

3. What is an example of a song that is not suitable for exercising?

_____

CRITICAL THINKING Reflecting   When you exercise, do you prefer listening to songs in English or in your own language? Note your answer and reasons below. Include examples of songs. Then discuss with a partner.

_____

_____

VOCABULARY PRACTICE

COMPLETION **A.** Complete the paragraph with words from the box. One word is used twice.

> beat   energy   range   seems   steady

Much of the research done on music and exercise focuses on what the ideal BPM

¹_____ is for running. But it also ²_____ from recent

studies that having a predictable, ³_____ rhythm is important. Generally,

music with sudden changes in the ⁴_____, like free-form jazz, is less

suitable. Why? If the music speed changes while we run, we tend to adjust our

movements to match the ⁵_____. Each time we change our steps to

move faster or slower, we lose ⁶_____.

COMPLETION **B.** Complete the sentences using words or phrases from the box.

> control   distract   pay attention   mood   social

1. Music can sometimes _____ you from
   your work.

2. Many people say that listening to the song "Happy" by
   Pharrell Williams puts them in a good _____.

3. If you want to have better _____ of your
   singing voice, you should do more vocal exercises.

4. Most schools organize _____ events like
   dances and concerts for the students.

5. Orchestra musicians must _____ to the
   conductor during a performance.

∧ **Pharrell's "Happy"
was the best-selling
song of 2014 in the
United States.**

COLLOCATIONS **C.** The prepositions in the box are often used with the word **control**. Complete
the definitions below with the correct prepositions.

> in   out of   under

1. If you are _____ control of a company, you have the power to make
   important decisions about the way it is run.

2. If a situation is _____ control, it is being dealt with successfully and is
   unlikely to cause any problems.

3. If something is _____ control, it cannot be dealt with successfully.

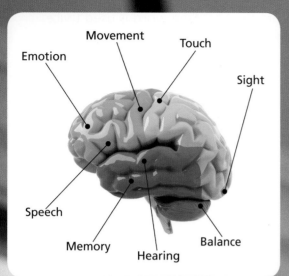

Emotion
Movement
Touch
Sight
Speech
Memory
Hearing
Balance

For most activities, we use several functions, or abilities, controlled by different parts of our brain.

BEFORE YOU READ

DISCUSSION **A.** Discuss the following questions with a partner.

1. Look at the brain diagram and the caption above. Which function(s) do you use when you sing? Play an instrument? Listen to music?

2. In what ways do you think music and language are similar?

PREDICTING **B.** Look at the reading title. What do you think *boost* means?

a. a change for the better

b. a problem

c. a system

Check your answer as you read the passage.

A MUSICAL BOOST

A Is there a **connection** between music and language? According to recent studies, the answer is yes: Music boosts **certain** language abilities in the brain. Here are two examples.

Music and Hearing

B A study from Northwestern University shows that playing a musical instrument can **improve** a person's hearing ability. As a part of the study, two groups of people listened to a person talking in a noisy room. The people in the first group were musicians, while those in the second group had no musical training. The musicians were able to hear the talking person more clearly.

C Musicians hear better, says study leader Nina Kraus, because they learn to pay attention to certain sounds. Think about violinists in an orchestra. When the violinists play with the group, they hear their own instrument and many others, too. But the violinists must listen closely to what they are playing, and **ignore** the other sounds. In this way, musicians are able to **concentrate** on certain sounds, even in a room with lots of noise.

Music and Speech

D Gottfried Schlaug, a doctor at Harvard Medical School, works with stroke[1] patients. Because of their illness, these people cannot say their names, addresses, or other information **normally**. However, they can still sing. Dr. Schlaug was surprised to find that singing words helped his patients to eventually speak. Why does this work? Schlaug isn't sure. Music seems to activate[2] different parts of the brain, including the **damaged** parts. This somehow helps patients use those parts of the brain again.

Understanding the Results

E Music improves concentration, memory, listening **skills**, and our **overall** language abilities. It can even help sick people get better. Playing an instrument or singing, says Nina Kraus, can help us do better in school and keep our brains **sharp** as we get older. Music, therefore, is not only enjoyable; it's also good for us in many other ways.

---

1 A **stroke** is an illness of the brain. It can make a person unable to move one side of their body.
2 If you **activate** something, you make it start working.

A. Choose the best answer for each question.

GIST **1.** What could be another title for the "Music and Hearing" section?

    a. Trained to Listen
    b. How to Be a Musician
    c. Playing in an Orchestra

DETAIL **2.** What two groups did Nina Kraus study?

    a. noisy people and quiet people
    b. musicians and nonmusicians
    c. violinists and other musicians

REFERENCE **3.** What does *they* refer to in paragraph C, line 3?

    a. orchestra musicians
    b. instruments
    c. violinists

∧ **Studies have suggested that playing classical music to babies may make them smarter.**

DETAIL **4.** What is true about Nina Kraus and Gottfried Schlaug?

    a. They both work at Harvard Medical School.
    b. They both play an instrument in an orchestra.
    c. They are both interested in how music and the brain are connected.

DETAIL **5.** How does Gottfried Schlaug help stroke patients speak?

    a. by playing music for them
    b. by getting them to sing words
    c. by teaching them to play instruments

EVALUATING STATEMENTS **B. Are the following statements true or false according to the reading passage, or is the information not given? Circle T (true), F (false), or NG (not given).**

1. In the Northwestern University study, the nonmusicians could hear better.   T   F   NG

2. Nina Kraus can play the violin very well.   T   F   NG

3. People who speak well can learn to play an instrument quickly.   T   F   NG

4. Gottfried Schlaug isn't sure why music helps stroke patients.   T   F   NG

5. Studies show that listening to music helps people sleep better.   T   F   NG

6. Nina Kraus believes that singing lessons can help students get better grades in school.   T   F   NG

Identifying Supporting Reasons (1)

Reasons are a type of supporting detail (see Unit 3A Reading Skill). A text may contain one or more reasons why something happens. Identifying *why* things happen helps you better understand the relationship between things in the text. The reason may appear before or after the action or effect. Words or phrases that signal reasons include *because* (*of*), *since*, and *due to*. In the following examples, the reason is underlined.

Musicians hear better because <u>they learn to pay attention to certain sounds</u>.

Singing words may help stroke patients since <u>this activates a different part of the brain</u>.

Because of <u>this need to concentrate</u>, musicians hear many sounds more clearly.

NOTICING **A.** Read the passage below. Circle the words or phrases that signal reasons.

Cameroon

How has Western music reached almost every corner of the world? Researchers believe Western music is popular because of its ability to express emotions across cultures.

Researcher Tom Fritz played parts of 42 Western songs to members of the Mafa, an ethnic group in Cameroon. Since he wanted to include a variety of Western music types, Fritz played classical, rock, pop, and jazz. He asked the group members to point to pictures of people's faces to show the emotion the music expressed.

The Mafa were able to identify the emotions correctly. This was probably due to the fact that the rhythms and melodies of Western music are similar to those of basic human speech. So some part of the way we understand Western music is shared by everyone, regardless of our own cultures.

SUPPORTING REASONS **B.** Answer these questions with the supporting reasons from the passage.

1. Why do researchers believe Western music is popular?

_____

2. Why did Tom Fritz play classical, rock, pop, and jazz music?

_____

3. Why were the Mafa able to identify the emotions correctly?

_____

CRITICAL THINKING Relating to Personal Experience   Does listening to music help you study or concentrate? If so, what kinds of music help you? What other factors might help you concentrate better? Note your answers and share them with a partner.

_____

_____

VOCABULARY PRACTICE

WORDS IN CONTEXT **A.** Complete each sentence with the correct answer (a or b).

1. If you **ignore** something, you _____ it.
   a. don't pay attention to   b. focus on

2. A **certain** sound refers to _____ type of sound.
   a. only one   b. any

3. If you **concentrate**, you _____.
   a. think very hard   b. don't think at all

4. Two examples of **skills** are _____.
   a. food and drink   b. cooking and sewing

5. A person's **overall** abilities means their abilities _____.
   a. related to a single skill   b. as a whole

COMPLETION **B.** Complete the paragraph with words from the box.

^ **Dr. Oliver Sacks (1933–2015)**

| connection | damaged | improved | normally | sharp |

In his book *Musicophilia*, brain scientist Dr. Oliver Sacks looked at the
¹_____ between music and the brain. He wrote about how music
²_____ the lives of musicians, hospital patients, and ordinary people.
Dr. Sacks also shared the experiences of different people. He gave an example of a man
whose brain was ³_____ by a lightning strike, which—strangely—left
him wishing to become a musician at age 42. Another interesting example was of a
man whose memory ⁴_____ lasted only seven seconds, except when he
listened to music. When this happened, his mind became very ⁵_____,
with a near-perfect memory.

WORD FORMS **C.** We can add *-ion* to some verbs to form nouns (e.g., **connect** + *-ion* = **connection**).
Complete the sentences below using the verbs in the box. One verb is extra.

| act | connect | discuss | react |

1. Scientists still have a lot to learn about the _____**ion** between
language and music.

2. The new Taylor Swift song has received mixed _____**ions**.

3. The issue of music education in schools is a major topic of _____**ion**
these days.

> Classical musicians perform at a restaurant in Moscow.

THE MOZART EFFECT

BEFORE YOU WATCH

PREVIEWING **A.** Read the information. The words and phrases in **bold** appear in the video. Match these words and phrases with their definitions (1–3).

Many people enjoy listening to classical music (e.g., the music of Mozart). There have been claims that listening to classical music makes you smarter and raises **IQ**. This theory is called the "Mozart Effect." To test this theory, University of Virginia psychologist Dr. Jim Coan carried out an **experiment**. He gave people some word puzzles and asked them if they could **figure out** the answers, both before and after listening to classical music. What do you think the results showed? Can classical music make people smarter? Dr. Coan's findings may surprise you.

1. _____ : to understand or solve something

2. _____ : a number that represents a person's level of intelligence

3. _____ : a scientific test done in order to learn something

QUIZ **B.** In the video, Dr. Coan uses word puzzles to test people's IQ (e.g., "7 DOTW" stands for "7 days of the week"). Can you figure out what these puzzles mean? Discuss with a partner.

- 12 MOTY
- 7 WOTW
- 24 HIAD
- 18 HOAGC

GIST **A.** Watch the video. Write the answers to the puzzles below. Were your answers in Before You Watch B correct?

- 12 MOTY = _____
- 7 WOTW = _____
- 24 HIAD = _____
- 18 HOAGC = _____

MULTIPLE CHOICE **B.** Watch the video again. Choose the correct answer for each question.

1. Most of the people in the experiment _____ after listening to classical music.

a. did better　　　　　　　b. showed no change

2. What other kind of music (besides classical music) did the people in the video listen to?

a. hip-hop music　　　　　b. rock music

3. Which of these statements summarizes Dr. Coan's findings?

a. Classical music is more effective than other kinds of music at improving people's focus and problem-solving abilities.

b. Any kind of music can improve people's reasoning abilities, as long as they enjoy listening to it.

CRITICAL THINKING Evaluating Methods　Discuss these questions with a partner.

▶ Can you think of any weaknesses in Dr. Coan's methods? What are some other possible reasons for people's improved performance in his experiment?

▶ Can you think of a better way to test the Mozart Effect? Plan your own experiment.

VOCABULARY REVIEW

Do you remember the meanings of these words? Check (✓) the ones you know. Look back at the unit and review any words you're not sure of.

Reading A

☐ beat	☐ control	☐ distract	☐ energy*	☐ mood
☐ pay attention	☐ range*	☐ seem	☐ social	☐ steady

Reading B

☐ certain	☐ concentrate*	☐ connection	☐ damaged	☐ ignore*
☐ improve	☐ normally*	☐ overall*	☐ sharp	☐ skill

* Academic Word List

INTO SPACE

4

Astronaut David A. Wolf
takes a spacewalk outside the
International Space Station.

WARM UP

Discuss these questions
with a partner.

1. What movies or TV
   shows about space have
   you seen? Describe them.

2. Do you think there is life
   in outer space? Why or
   why not?

The Kepler Space Telescope was sent off into space in 2009. Named after Johannes Kepler—a German astronomer from the 17th century—it discovered over 2,600 **planets** during its lifetime. As a result, scientists now believe that there are probably more planets than stars in our **galaxy**.

BEFORE YOU READ

DEFINITIONS

A. Read the caption above and match the words in **bold** with their definitions (1–4).

1. Mars, Jupiter, and Earth are all _____.

2. A(n) _____ is a very large group of stars, gas, and dust.

3. A(n) _____ makes distant objects appear closer.

4. A(n) _____ studies stars and other objects in space.

SKIMMING

Review this reading skill in Unit 1A

B. Skim the passage quickly. What do Shostak and Barnett think?

a. We might soon communicate with beings from space.

b. We will probably never find intelligent life outside Earth.

c. We have probably already contacted beings from space.

Check your answer as you read.

LIFE
BEYOND
EARTH?

A Is there intelligent life on other planets besides Earth? For years, scientists weren't sure. Today, this is changing. Seth Shostak and Alexandra Barnett are astronomers. They believe intelligent life **exists** elsewhere in the universe.[1] They also think we will soon **contact** these beings.[2]

B Why do these astronomers think intelligent life exists on other planets? The first reason is time. Scientists believe the universe is about 12 billion years old. According to Shostak and Barnett, this is too long a period for only one planet in the **whole** universe to develop intelligent life. The second reason is size—the universe is huge. **Tools** such as the Hubble Telescope have shown that "there are at least 100 billion … galaxies," says Shostak. And our galaxy—the Milky Way— has at least 100 billion stars. Some planets that **circle** these stars might be similar to Earth.

---

1 The **universe** is all of space—all the stars, planets, and other objects.
2 A person or a living creature (e.g., an animal) is a **being**.

Looking for Intelligent Life

C Until recently, it was difficult to **search** for signs of intelligent life in the universe. But now, **powerful** telescopes **allow** scientists to **identify** many more small planets—the size of Mars or Earth—in other solar systems.[3] If these planets are similar to Earth and are close enough to a star, they might have intelligent life.

Making Contact

D Have beings from outer space already visited Earth? Probably not, says Shostak. The **distance** between planets is too great. Despite this, intelligent beings might eventually contact us using other methods, such as radio signals[4] or flashes of light.[5] In fact, they could be trying to communicate with us now, but we may not have the right tools to receive their messages. This is changing, however, says Shostak. He predicts that we will make contact with other life forms in our universe within the next 20 years.

---

3 The **solar system** is made up of the sun and all the planets that orbit around it.

4 A **radio signal** is a way of sending information using radio waves.

5 A **flash of light** is a sudden, short burst of bright light.

< Scientists are hoping to build spaceships that could reach the closest stars.

A. Choose the best answer for each question.

PURPOSE

1. What is the main purpose of this reading?

a. to discuss how life probably started on Earth
b. to explain why we might find intelligent life outside of Earth
c. to describe what life on other planets might look like

DETAIL

2. Which possible reason for the existence of intelligent life is NOT mentioned?

a. Some planets that circle stars might be similar to Earth.
b. The universe is too old to have just one planet with intelligent life.
c. Some other planets in the Milky Way have water.

DETAIL

3. According to the reading passage, why was it difficult to search for signs of intelligent life in the past?

a. Telescopes weren't powerful enough.
b. The distance between planets was too great.
c. There were too few trained astronomers.

VOCABULARY

4. What does *life forms* in the last sentence of the passage mean?

a. messages   b. beings   c. planets

DETAIL

5. Why does Shostak think we will make contact with intelligent life within the next 20 years?

a. We will have better technology to receive their messages.
b. Bigger telescopes will identify more planets like Earth.
c. Intelligent life will finally receive messages that we send to them.

SHORT ANSWER

B. Write short answers for these questions. Use information from the reading passage.

1. What tool has been used to discover billions of galaxies?

_____

2. Does Shostak think that beings from other planets have visited Earth?

_____

3. Besides radio signals, what else could other life forms use to contact us?

_____

NASA has found what looks like a large moon > orbiting a planet outside our solar system. This could be the first known alien moon.

Summarizing: Using a Concept Map

When you summarize a text, you record the main ideas and key details. A concept map can help you organize these ideas in a clear and logical way, and can help you understand information better. In a concept map, the main ideas are linked by words and phrases that explain the connection between them.

You can create a concept map by first starting with a main idea, topic, or issue. Then note the key concepts that link to this main idea. The bigger and more general concepts come first, which are then linked to smaller, more specific concepts.

ANALYZING   **A.** Look back at Reading A. Find the main ideas and key details in the text.

SUMMARIZING   **B.** Complete the concept map below with words or phrases from Reading A.

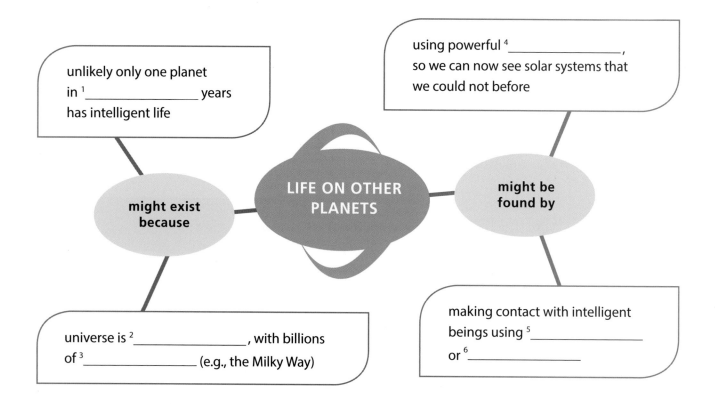

unlikely only one planet in ¹_____ years has intelligent life

using powerful ⁴_____, so we can now see solar systems that we could not before

might exist because

LIFE ON OTHER PLANETS

might be found by

universe is ²_____, with billions of ³_____ (e.g., the Milky Way)

making contact with intelligent beings using ⁵_____ or ⁶_____

CRITICAL THINKING Speculating   Imagine a space station receives a radio signal from another planet confirming intelligent life there. What do you think would happen next? Discuss with a partner and note your ideas.

_____

_____

VOCABULARY PRACTICE

COMPLETION   **A.** Circle the correct words to complete the paragraph below.

Is there life on other planets? Scientists use different methods to try to answer this question. Some use very ¹**powerful / whole** radio telescopes. They hope to receive messages from intelligent life on distant planets. Other scientists only ²**search / contact** for life in our solar system. But they aren't looking for intelligent life—they want to ³**circle / identify** any possible life forms. To do this, they test whether conditions on a planet would ⁴**allow / contact** any kind of life to ⁵**exist / search**.

WORDS IN CONTEXT   **B.** Complete each sentence with the correct answer (a or b).

1. We measure **distance** in _____ .
   a. kilometers (km)
   b. kilograms (kg)

2. Some examples of **tools** are _____ .
   a. monkeys and dolphins
   b. cell phones and laptops

3. If you **contact** someone, you _____ them.
   a. meet or communicate with
   b. research and write about

4. If you have lived in a place your **whole** life, you have lived there _____ of your life.
   a. some
   b. all

5. If a spaceship **circles** a planet, it _____ the planet.
   a. goes around
   b. lands on

▲ **The SpaceX Falcon Heavy rocket lifted off on February 6, 2018.**

WORD PARTS   **C.** The suffix *-ful* in **powerful** means "full of." Complete the sentences using the words in the box. One word is extra.

care	harm	power	wonder

1. Moon dust can be _____**ful** and can damage our DNA.
2. Astronomers need to be very _____**ful** with the expensive equipment they use.
3. The Falcon Heavy rocket is extremely _____**ful**. It can carry a load of 60,000 kg.

4B

BEFORE YOU READ

COMPLETION **A.** Read these definitions. Then complete the paragraph below with the correct form of the words in **bold**.

astronaut: a person who travels into space

colony: a place under the control of another place, usually another country

establish: to make or start something (e.g., a system or an organization)

rocket: a vehicle used to travel to space

Robert Zubrin is a(n) ¹_____ scientist; he designs spaceships. He thinks we should send a group of ²_____ into space, but not just to visit. Zubrin wants to ³_____ a human ⁴_____ on Mars. He wants to change the planet into a new place for humans to live.

PREDICTING **B.** Read the sentence below. Circle your answer and complete the sentence. Then compare your ideas with those in the passage.

Sending humans into space to live *is / is not* a good idea because

_____

_____.

▲ **This is what a colony on Mars might look like in the future.**

LIVING IN SPACE

A Stephen Hawking, one of the world's most famous scientists, believed that to survive, humans will one day have to move into space. "Once we spread out into space and establish **independent** colonies, our future should be safe," he said.

B Today, the United States, Europe, Russia, China, and Japan are all planning to send astronauts back to Earth's closest **neighbor**: the moon. Some of these countries want to create space stations there within the next 10 years. These stations will prepare humans to visit and later live on Mars or other Earthlike planets.

C Robert Zubrin, a rocket scientist, thinks humans should colonize space. He wants to start with Mars. Why? He thinks sending people to Mars will allow us to learn a lot of things—for example, the ability of humans to live in a very different **environment**. Eventually, we could create new human societies on other planets. In addition, any **advances** we make in the fields of science, technology, **medicine**, and health will **benefit** people here on Earth.

D SpaceX is a company that builds rockets. Its founder and CEO, Elon Musk, also believes we should colonize Mars. He doesn't want to send just "one little **mission**," though. His long-term goal is to put one million people on the planet in case something bad happens to us here on Earth.

E Not everyone thinks sending humans into space is a smart idea. Many say it's too expensive. Also, most space trips are not short. A one-way trip to Mars, for example, would take at least six months. People traveling this kind of distance could face many health problems. In addition, these first people would find life extremely difficult in space. On the moon's **surface**, for example, the sun's rays[1] are very dangerous. People would have to stay indoors most of the time.

F Despite these **concerns**, sending people into space seems certain. In the future, we might see lunar[2] cities or even new human **cultures** on other planets. First stop: the moon.

---

1 The **sun's rays** are narrow beams of light from the sun.
2 **Lunar** means "related to the moon."

A. Choose the best answer for each question.

PURPOSE

1. What is the main purpose of this passage?

   a. to give reasons for and against space colonization
   b. to describe what life would be like on the moon
   c. to compare the environments of Mars and the moon

REFERENCE

2. What does *our* in Stephen Hawking's quote "our future should be safe" (paragraph A) refer to?

   a. scientists'
   b. humans'
   c. colonies'

DETAIL

3. Why are some countries planning to build lunar space stations?

   a. to learn more about the moon's surface
   b. to reduce the number of people living on Earth
   c. to prepare humans to live on other planets

DETAIL

4. Which reason for living in space is NOT mentioned?

   a. We can learn if humans can live in a very different environment from that of Earth.
   b. We can establish human societies on other planets besides Earth.
   c. We can search for signs of intelligent life elsewhere in the universe.

▲ **A Japanese food company has developed vacuum-packed ramen noodles that can be eaten easily in space.**

PARAPHRASE

5. What does *First stop: the moon* mean in the last sentence?

   a. Everybody wants to visit the moon first.
   b. All spaceships to other planets have to stop at the moon first.
   c. The first human colony in space will likely be on the moon.

MAIN IDEA

Review this reading skill in Unit 1B

B. Match each paragraph with its main idea.

1. Paragraph B •

2. Paragraph C •

3. Paragraph D •

4. Paragraph E •

• a. There are several reasons not to send humans to space.

• b. A mission to Mars should be designed on a large scale.

• c. Many countries are planning missions to the moon and beyond.

• d. There are a number of reasons to travel to Mars.

Identifying Supporting Reasons (2)

A reading text will sometimes contain arguments for and against an idea. It can be useful to identify and list all the reasons for and against an idea. This can help you form your own opinion on a particular topic.

ANALYZING **A.** Look back at Reading B. Read paragraph C and recall its main idea. Then underline the reasons that support the main idea.

COMPLETION **B.** Now read paragraph E of Reading B. Complete the concept map below by writing the reasons in the boxes.

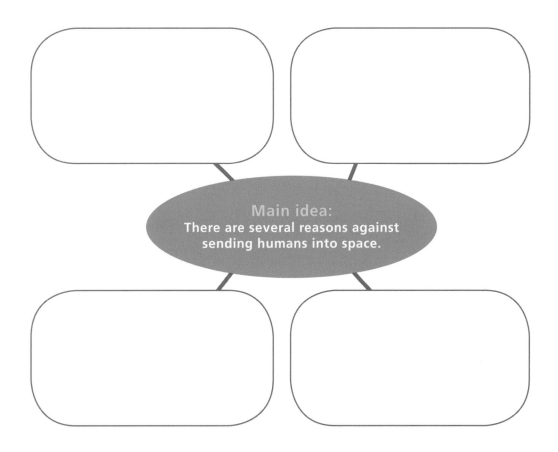

Main idea:
There are several reasons against sending humans into space.

CRITICAL THINKING Reflecting

▶ Imagine you have a chance to join a new colony on Mars. Would you go? Why or why not? Note your answer and reasons below.

_____

_____

▶ Compare your reasons above with your answers in Before You Read B (on page 56). Has Reading B changed your opinion in any way? Discuss with a partner.

DEFINITIONS **A.** Read the paragraph and match each word in **red** with its definition (1–5).

A **mission** to our planetary **neighbor** Mars would take at least a year—six months to get there and six months to return. This sounds like a long time. But what's more difficult than getting to Mars is actually living there. People who want to live in this **environment** would need water to survive, and they would probably have to take it with them from Earth. Recently, however, scientists found signs of a large body of liquid water under the **surface** of the planet. If confirmed, it would make people on Mars more **independent** from Earth.

1. _____ : able to live on one's own

2. _____ : the outer part of something

3. _____ : a special trip that has an aim or a goal

4. _____ : a person, country, or thing located nearby

5. _____ : the things and conditions around a person, animal, or plant

WORDS IN CONTEXT **B.** Complete each sentence with the correct answer (a or b).

1. A student of **medicine** probably wants to be a(n) _____.

a. doctor   b. astronaut

2. A person's **culture** includes _____.

a. their way of life   b. how they breathe

3. If we make **advances** in science or technology, we _____ in those areas.

a. do worse   b. improve

4. If something **benefits** you, it _____ you.

a. helps   b. hurts

5. A **concern** is a fact or situation that _____ you.

a. surprises   b. worries

△ **Water-ice clouds drift over the surface of Mars.**

COLLOCATIONS **C.** The words in the box are often used with the word **environment**. Complete the sentences with the correct words from the box.

| safe | unfamiliar | work |

1. "Culture shock" is a common reaction to moving to a new, _____ environment.

2. My colleagues have tried to create a friendly _____ environment.

3. Every child has the right to grow up in a(n) _____ environment.

Sunset over Mars

VIDEO

THE RED PLANET

BEFORE YOU WATCH

PREVIEWING **A.** Read the information. The words in **bold** appear in the video. Match these words with their definitions (1–3).

Mars—otherwise known as "the Red Planet"—has fascinated scientists for a long time. With a diameter[1] of 6,778 km, it is about half the size of Earth. The air on Mars would kill a human quickly, and its surface is dry and **barren**. However, some scientists think life existed there in the past—and may exist again. They believe that we will all have to leave Earth one day, so they hope to **launch** manned missions to Mars and form a colony there. For these scientists, Mars might be the key to the survival of **humanity**.

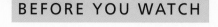

1 The **diameter** of a round object is the length of a straight line that can be drawn across it, passing through the center.

1. _____ : all people on Earth

2. _____ : unable to produce plants or fruit

3. _____ : to send into the air or into space

QUIZ **B.** Read the sentences below and guess if they are correct. Circle **T** (true) or **F** (false).

1. Mars is more than five billion years old. T F

2. Mars is named after the Roman god of love. T F

3. Mars has the largest volcano in the solar system. T F

4. The volcanoes on Mars are still active. T F

GIST **A.** Watch the video. Check your answers in Before You Watch B.

COMPLETION **B.** Watch the video again. Complete this concept map.

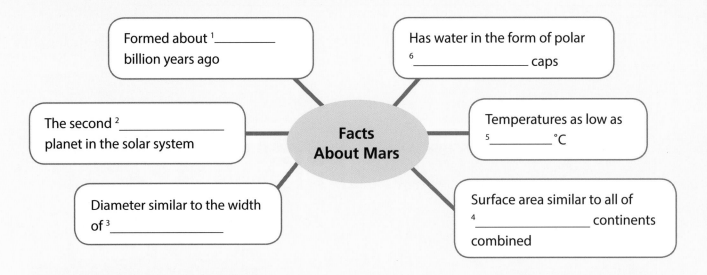

Formed about [1]_____ billion years ago

Has water in the form of polar [6]_____ caps

The second [2]_____ planet in the solar system

Facts About Mars

Temperatures as low as [5]_____ °C

Diameter similar to the width of [3]_____

Surface area similar to all of [4]_____ continents combined

CRITICAL THINKING Ranking Tasks Imagine you are one of the first people to colonize Mars. How important would these tasks be for your colony? Rank them 1–4 (1 = most important; 4 = least important). Then compare answers with a partner and give reasons.

_____ setting up a fast communication channel with Earth

_____ developing a spacesuit that is easy to wear and move around in

_____ establishing an effective heating system to keep people's houses warm

_____ finding a way to grow fresh fruit and vegetables

VOCABULARY REVIEW

Do you remember the meanings of these words? Check (✓) the ones you know. Look back at the unit and review any words you're not sure of.

Reading A

☐ allow   ☐ circle   ☐ contact*   ☐ distance   ☐ exist

☐ identify* ☐ powerful   ☐ search   ☐ tool   ☐ whole

Reading B

☐ advance   ☐ benefit*   ☐ concern   ☐ culture*   ☐ environment*

☐ independent ☐ medicine   ☐ mission   ☐ neighbor   ☐ surface

* Academic Word List

5

CITY LIFE

WARM UP

Discuss these questions with
a partner.

1. Why do you think so many people
   choose to live in cities?

2. What are some of the world's most
   important cities? Why are they
   important?

The mirrored entrance to Tokyu
Plaza Omotesando Harajuku
reflects the busy streets of Tokyo.

A gargoyle on Notre-Dame
Cathedral looks out over Paris.

BEFORE YOU READ

DISCUSSION **A.** Study the graph on the next page and
discuss these questions with a partner.

1. Have you been to any of the cities listed
on the graph? What were they like?

2. How are the top four cities similar to
and different from one another?

PREDICTING **B.** Which other cities do you think will
become important in the future? Why?
Discuss with a partner. Then check your
ideas as you read the passage.

GLOBAL CITIES

A "New York City is a star—the city of cities," wrote author John Gunther. But what makes a city great? To answer this question, the creators of the Global Cities Index looked at the following:

- **Business** – How many global companies are in the city? Does the city do a lot of **international** business?

- **People** – Does the city **attract** talented[1] people from around the world? Are the city's universities good? How many residents have college degrees?

- **Media** – Is it easy to get information from different **sources** (TV, radio, Internet)? How many residents have Internet **access**?

- **Entertainment** – Does the city have many entertainment **options**: museums, sports, music, and different types of restaurants?

- **Politics** – How many embassies[2] and international **organizations** are in the city?

---

1 A **talented** person has special skills and can do something well.
2 An **embassy** is a government building where officials from a foreign country work.

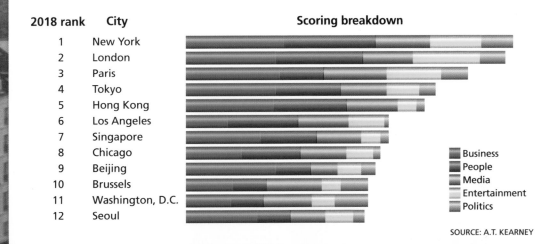

The Global Cities Index is a list of the world's most powerful and important cities. The top 12 cities in 2018 are listed here.

2018 rank	City	Scoring breakdown
1	New York	
2	London	
3	Paris	
4	Tokyo	
5	Hong Kong	
6	Los Angeles	
7	Singapore	
8	Chicago	
9	Beijing	
10	Brussels	
11	Washington, D.C.	
12	Seoul	

Legend: Business, People, Media, Entertainment, Politics

SOURCE: A.T. KEARNEY

Future Leaders

B As the graph on the previous page shows, most cities on the Global Cities Index are strong in certain areas. Beijing's strength, for example, is business, while Los Angeles's strength is people. New York, London, and Paris are at the top because they are strong in all five areas.

C Which cities will become more powerful in the future? Creators of the Global Cities Index **predict** the most growth in the following places:

- **Asia:** Beijing and Shanghai are both business centers and will continue to grow. In a few years, they will be as powerful as New York. Other Chinese cities such as Guangzhou and Shenzhen will also grow. Indian cities such as Mumbai and New Delhi have a lot of business **potential**, too.

- **South America:** Rio de Janeiro and São Paulo in Brazil, Buenos Aires in Argentina, and Bogotá in Colombia will become more powerful. In these cities, the middle class[3] is growing, and life for many people is improving.

- **The Middle East:** Istanbul in Turkey, Cairo in Egypt, and the cities of the United Arab Emirates (UAE) such as Dubai and Abu Dhabi will hold more power in international **politics** and business—**especially** in helping East and West work together.

D In 10 years, the top cities on the index may be different, but one thing is certain: With over 50 percent of the world's people now living in urban areas, tomorrow's global cities will be more powerful than ever.

---

3 The **middle class** is a category of people. They earn more than the working class, but less than the upper class. It includes professionals and business people.

∨ **An evening view of central Cairo**

A. Choose the best answer for each question.

GIST **1.** What is the reading mainly about?

    a. why certain global cities are important

    b. daily life in the world's fastest-growing cities

    c. Asian cities that will be important in 10 years

DETAIL **2.** What is NOT considered in the Global Cities Index?

    a. food

    b. weather

    c. education

DETAIL **3.** According to the reading, which part of the world is predicted to grow in the area of politics?

    a. Asia

    b. South America

    c. the Middle East

VOCABULARY **4.** In paragraph D, what does *urban* refer to?

    a. cities and towns

    b. the future

    c. the globe

INFERENCE **5.** Which statement would the writer probably agree with?

    a. A top global city needs to be strong in several areas.

    b. The Global Cities Index will probably list the same top cities 10 years from now.

    c. Tomorrow's global cities will probably be less powerful than today's.

SUMMARIZING **B. Complete the concept map with words or phrases from the reading.**

Review this reading skill in Unit 4A

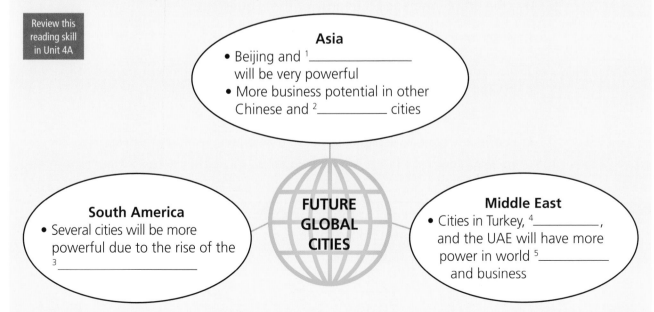

Asia
- Beijing and 1_____ will be very powerful
- More business potential in other Chinese and 2_____ cities

FUTURE GLOBAL CITIES

South America
- Several cities will be more powerful due to the rise of the 3_____

Middle East
- Cities in Turkey, 4_____, and the UAE will have more power in world 5_____ and business

Understanding Charts and Graphs

Charts and graphs may contain important details not mentioned in the text. One of the most common types of graphs is the bar graph. A bar graph uses either horizontal bars going across (the *x*-axis) or vertical bars going up (the *y*-axis) to show comparisons among categories. For example:

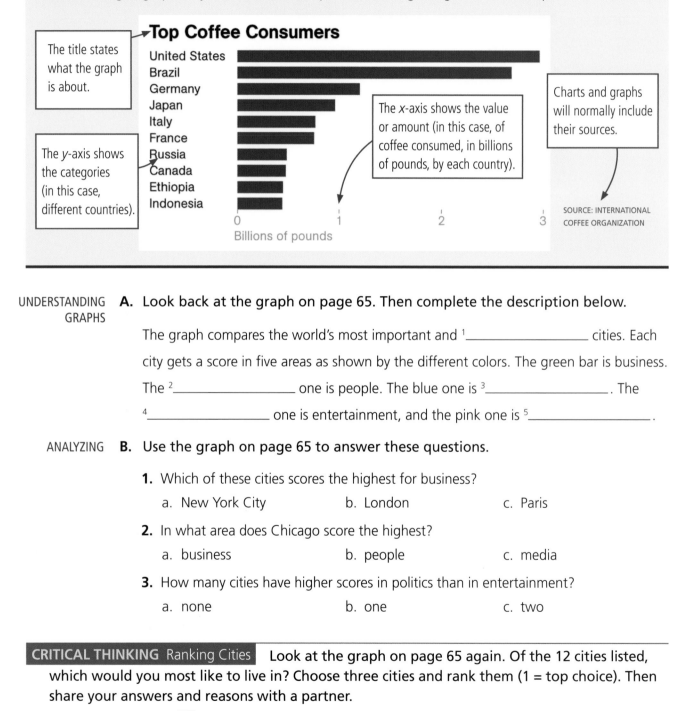

The title states what the graph is about.

Top Coffee Consumers

The *y*-axis shows the categories (in this case, different countries).

The *x*-axis shows the value or amount (in this case, of coffee consumed, in billions of pounds, by each country).

Charts and graphs will normally include their sources.

United States
Brazil
Germany
Japan
Italy
France
Russia
Canada
Ethiopia
Indonesia

0   1   2   3

Billions of pounds

SOURCE: INTERNATIONAL COFFEE ORGANIZATION

UNDERSTANDING GRAPHS

A. **Look back at the graph on page 65. Then complete the description below.**

The graph compares the world's most important and ¹_____ cities. Each city gets a score in five areas as shown by the different colors. The green bar is business. The ²_____ one is people. The blue one is ³_____. The ⁴_____ one is entertainment, and the pink one is ⁵_____.

ANALYZING

B. **Use the graph on page 65 to answer these questions.**

1. Which of these cities scores the highest for business?
   a. New York City   b. London   c. Paris

2. In what area does Chicago score the highest?
   a. business   b. people   c. media

3. How many cities have higher scores in politics than in entertainment?
   a. none   b. one   c. two

CRITICAL THINKING Ranking Cities   Look at the graph on page 65 again. Of the 12 cities listed, which would you most like to live in? Choose three cities and rank them (1 = top choice). Then share your answers and reasons with a partner.

1. _____   2. _____   3. _____

DEFINITIONS

A. Read the paragraph and match each word in **red** with its definition (1–5).

Times Square in New York City **attracts** about 50 million people every year, including many **international** tourists. It has a huge variety of entertainment **options** such as movie theaters, restaurants, and shopping. It is **especially** famous for its Broadway shows. City officials **predict** that Times Square will remain the most visited tourist spot in the United States for years to come.

1. _____ : choices
2. _____ : in particular
3. _____ : pulls; draws in
4. _____ : involving two or more countries
5. _____ : to say that something will happen in the future

⌃ **Times Square, New York City**

WORDS IN CONTEXT

B. Complete each sentence with the correct answer (a or b).

1. If you have **access** to something, you have _____ .
   a. a list of reasons to support it   b. a way to get or use it

2. An example of an **organization** is _____ .
   a. a teacher   b. the United Nations

3. Someone who is interested in **politics** is probably interested in _____ .
   a. how people choose their leaders   b. what websites people visit

4. If someone has **potential**, they have an ability that _____ be developed.
   a. can   b. cannot

5. Examples of **sources** of information might be _____ .
   a. questions and ideas   b. newspapers and websites

WORD PARTS

C. The prefix *inter-* means "between" or "among" (e.g., *inter-* + *national* = **international**). Complete the sentences using the words in the box.

national	net	section

1. Many people today cannot imagine their lives without the **Inter**_____ .
2. Beijing has one of the world's busiest **inter**_____ airports.
3. New York's Times Square is located at the **inter**_____ of Broadway and Seventh Avenue.

BEFORE YOU READ

DEFINITIONS **A.** Read this paragraph and match each word in **bold** with its definition (1–3).

Every year, millions of people leave their country and **settle** in another one. In some cities, **immigrants** from a particular country live or shop in the same **neighborhood** (e.g., Chinatown in London).

1. _____ : an area in a city where people live

2. _____ : to go and live somewhere for a long time

3. _____ : people who have come to a foreign country to live

PREDICTING **B.** The reading passage discusses immigrants in São Paulo (Brazil) and Hamamatsu (Japan). What do you think is the connection between these two cities? Check your ideas as you read.

Residents celebrate a
traditional Japanese festival
in Liberdade, São Paulo, Brazil.

A TASTE OF TWO CITIES

A The city of São Paulo, Brazil, has hundreds of Japanese restaurants. A world away, in Hamamatsu, Japan, there are many places to buy and eat Brazilian food. Why is each country's food so **popular** in the other? The answer to this question dates back to the early 20th century.

B In 1908, people from Japan began moving to Brazil to work on coffee plantations.[1] Many of these Japanese immigrants (called *nikkei*) moved to São Paulo and settled in a neighborhood called Liberdade. Like many immigrants, they spoke their native language and prepared **traditional** foods from their home country. Over time, the *nikkei* opened many Japanese markets and restaurants in the Liberdade **district**. Today, this neighborhood has one of the largest Japanese **communities** outside of Japan. Restaurants sell ramen noodles and sushi on every corner. Also, each weekend, there is a large street market. Street sellers sell traditional Japanese **goods** and foods. The **event** is popular with both city residents and tourists.

Hamamatsu

PACIFIC OCEAN

São Paulo

C In the 1980s—three **generations** after the first *nikkei* settled in Brazil—a reverse migration began to take place. Over 300,000 Japanese-Brazilians moved to Japan, mainly to work in electronics and automobile factories. Many settled in Hamamatsu, a city on the east **coast** of Japan. Most Japanese-Brazilians spoke only their native language (Portuguese). They also missed the foods and culture of Brazil. Over time, a number of Brazilian restaurants and **stores** opened in Hamamatsu. Today, there is still a large Brazilian **population** in the city. All over Hamamatsu, food shops and restaurants sell traditional Brazilian foods, such as *pão de queijo* (a type of bread) and *feijoada* (a bean stew with beef and pork).

D Today, it's possible to eat excellent Japanese food in São Paulo and traditional Brazilian cuisine[2] in Hamamatsu. Whether traveling through Brazil or Japan, it's worth visiting these two cities to experience the tastes and cultures of their unique immigrant communities.

---

1 A **plantation** is a large farm on which crops such as coffee, tea, and sugar are grown.
2 **Cuisine** is a type of cooking (e.g., Brazilian cuisine, Italian cuisine).

A. Choose the best answer for each question.

PURPOSE

1. What is the main purpose of this passage?

    a. to discuss the challenges that immigrants face

    b. to explore the role of food in immigrant communities

    c. to compare immigration statistics in two different countries

DETAIL

2. The *nikkei* first came to Brazil ___.

    a. to grow coffee

    b. as tourists

    c. to open restaurants

DETAIL

3. Which sentence about the street market in Liberdade is NOT true?

    a. It is a popular tourist attraction.

    b. It is open every day.

    c. You can try traditional Japanese dishes there.

REFERENCE

4. What does *Many* refer to in paragraph C?

    a. many factories

    b. many Japanese-Brazilians

    c. many generations

INFERENCE

5. The author's suggestion in the last sentence is directed to ___.

    a. immigrants in general

    b. the *nikkei*

    c. tourists

EVALUATING STATEMENTS

B. Are the following statements true or false according to the reading passage, or is the information not given? Circle T (true), F (false), or NG (not given).

1. The *nikkei* opened Japanese schools in São Paulo.   T   F   NG

2. The main reason Japanese-Brazilians moved to Japan in the 1980s was to sell Brazilian goods.   T   F   NG

3. There is a large Brazilian street market in Hamamatsu every weekend.   T   F   NG

4. Many Japanese-Brazilians who moved to Japan in the 1980s and 1990s did not speak Japanese.   T   F   NG

5. *Feijoada* is a traditional Brazilian vegetarian dish.   T   F   NG

⌃ *Feijoada* **is often called the national dish of Brazil.**

Summarizing: Using a T-chart (1)

Instead of using a concept map to summarize the main ideas and supporting details from a text (see Unit 4A Reading Skill), you may choose to summarize information in a T-chart. A T-chart is especially useful when two things are discussed or compared, when a passage discusses the pros (advantages) and cons (disadvantages) of something, or when a passage provides the reasons for and against an argument.

ANALYZING **A.** Look back at Reading B. Underline the main ideas and key details in the text.

SUMMARIZING **B.** Complete the chart below with words or numbers from Reading B.

São Paulo, Brazil	Hamamatsu, Japan
In the past:	*In the past:*
• in 1908, many Japanese people began to move to Brazil to work on ¹_____ plantations	• in the ⁶_____, Japanese-Brazilians began to move to Japan (reverse migration) to work in electronics and car ⁷_____
• immigrants (called *nikkei*) settled in ²_____ (neighborhood)	• immigrants settled in Hamamatsu (city)
• spoke native language, ate foods from home country	• spoke native language (⁸_____), missed foods from home country
• opened Japanese ³_____ and restaurants	• opened Brazilian restaurants and stores
Today:	*Today:*
• very large Japanese community	• large Brazilian community
• Japanese foods (e.g., ramen and ⁴_____) widely available	• Brazilian foods (e.g., *pão de queijo*, a kind of ⁹_____) widely available
• Japanese street market each weekend; popular with locals and ⁵_____	

CRITICAL THINKING Relating Has your country's cuisine been influenced by foreign cuisines? How? Discuss with a partner and note your ideas. Include examples of dishes.

_____

_____

_____

COMPLETION **A.** Complete the paragraph with words from the box.

coast	district	goods	popular	stores	traditional

One of the most [1]_____ places for tourists to visit in Dubai is the Gold Souk, located in the Al Dhagaya [2]_____ on Dubai's northeastern [3]_____. In contrast to the city's modern shopping malls, the souk is a [4]_____ Arabian market. It has over 300 [5]_____ selling a wide range of gold jewelry and other [6]_____. The total weight of all the gold in the souk is believed to be about 10 tons— about the same as two full-grown elephants!

▲ **A jewelry seller working in Dubai's Gold Souk**

WORDS IN CONTEXT **B.** Complete each sentence with the correct answer (a or b).

1. The **population** of a country or an area is all the _____ in it.
   a. people b. buildings

2. An example of an important **event** is a _____.
   a. school b. sports competition

3. A **generation** is the period of time that it takes for children to _____.
   a. grow up and become adults b. learn how to read

4. A **community** is a group of people who _____ a particular area.
   a. visit b. live in

WORD FORMS **C.** We can add *-ation* to some verbs to form nouns (e.g., *generate* + *-ation* = **generation**). Use the noun form of these verbs to complete the sentences. One verb is extra.

communicate	generate	organize	populate

1. The total _____ of Brazil is over 211 million.
2. Listening is an important part of _____.
3. A(n) _____ ago, social media like Facebook and Twitter didn't exist.

One Bryant Park (center) is among New York City's tallest buildings.

NEW YORK SKYSCRAPER

BEFORE YOU WATCH

PREVIEWING   **A.** Read the information about One Bryant Park. Then discuss the questions (1–3) with a partner.

> **Name:** One Bryant Park (also known as the Bank of America Tower)
> **Year construction began:** 2004   **Year completed:** 2009
> **Height:** 288 meters   **Height including spire:** 366 meters
> **Number of floors:** 55   **Building cost:** $1 billion
> **Earth removed for foundation:** 198,000 cubic meters

1. How long did the building take to complete?
2. What part of the building do you think the spire is? How tall is the spire?
3. What part of the building do you think the foundation is?

PREDICTING   **B.** What do you think was challenging about building One Bryant Park? Discuss with a partner and note some ideas.

_____

_____

GIST **A.** Watch the video. Check (✓) the challenges of building a high-rise that the video discusses. Were any of your predictions in Before You Watch B mentioned in the video?

☐ a. digging the foundation   ☐ b. lifting materials up into the tower

☐ c. working in bad weather   ☐ d. driving big trucks through city traffic

COMPLETION **B.** Watch the video again. Circle the correct words to complete the sentences.

1. The crane operator is so high up that he is not able to *talk to the other workers / see what he is lifting*.

2. The workers have difficulty with the water tank because of its *large size / unusual shape*.

3. Michael Keen says that the city traffic "gets a little hairy at times." The word *hairy* probably means *dangerous / noisy*.

4. The building's spire is put together *on / above* the ground.

CRITICAL THINKING Evaluating Pros and Cons   What are some pros and cons of living in a city skyscraper like One Bryant Park? Discuss with a partner and complete this chart.

Pros	Cons

VOCABULARY REVIEW

Do you remember the meanings of these words? Check (✓) the ones you know. Look back at the unit and review any words you're not sure of.

Reading A

☐ access*	☐ attract	☐ especially	☐ international	☐ option*
☐ organization	☐ politics	☐ potential*	☐ predict*	☐ source*

Reading B

☐ coast	☐ community*	☐ district	☐ event	☐ generation*
☐ goods	☐ popular	☐ population	☐ store	☐ traditional*

* Academic Word List

BACKYARD DISCOVERIES

Discuss these questions with a partner.

1. What are some natural places near your home? How much time do you spend there?

2. What types of animals and plants can you find at these places?

∧ A young explorer photographs a fern plant in a Canadian forest.

BEFORE YOU READ

DEFINITIONS   **A.** Read the caption below. Match each word in **bold** with its definition (1–3).

    1. _____ : living things

    2. _____ : very small in size

    3. _____ : the upper layer of the ground in which plants grow

PREDICTING   **B.** Read paragraph A. Why do you think small organisms are important? Discuss with a partner. Then read the rest of the passage to check your ideas.

Around us there are millions of **tiny** plants, insects, fish, and other animals, but we often don't see them. Most of these **organisms** live in the **soil**, or (like the ones pictured) in the water. Some are only a millimeter in size.

IN ONE CUBIC FOOT

A In any environment—forest, mountain, water—you always see the big animals first: birds, mammals, fish. But under your feet, both on land and in the water, there are many smaller organisms: insects, tiny plants, miniature sea creatures. They may seem unimportant, but, in fact, these sea creatures and ground dwellers[1] are "the heart of life on Earth," according to naturalist E. O. Wilson. Without them, our world would be a very different place.

The Cycle of Life

B Most organisms on Earth live on the ground or just below it. Here, they are part of an important **cycle**. When plants and animals die, they fall to the ground. Later, tiny insects and other organisms **break down** the dead plant and animal **material**. This **process** eventually returns nutrients[2] to the soil and gives living plants energy. These plants can then help to **maintain** a healthy environment for humans and other animals.

---

1 A **dweller** is a person or thing that lives in a certain place.
2 **Nutrients** are substances (like vitamins) that help plants and animals grow.

Discoveries in a Cube

C Despite their importance, **scientists** know very little about most ground organisms. To learn more, photographer David Liittschwager went to different places around the world, including a forest and a coral reef. In each place, he put a green 30-centimeter cube on the ground or in the water. Then he and his **team** counted and photographed the organisms that lived in or moved through the cube. Often they **discovered** hundreds of organisms, some only a millimeter in size. "It was like finding little gems,"[3] he says.

3 **Gems** are beautiful stones used in jewelry.

˅ **Coral Reef**
Moorea, French Polynesia
Here, Liittschwager photographed over 600 creatures in the cube. The team identified as many as possible, but it was difficult. Many of the animals they found were new **species**.

˅ **Tropical Cloud Forest**
Monteverde, Costa Rica
There are many different types of plants in this **region**. Almost 125 species that live here are found nowhere else on Earth.

A. Choose the best answer for each question.

GIST

1. What could be another title for this reading?

a. Tiny Organisms Are Everywhere
b. Saving Small Animals
c. The Life of a Photographer

VOCABULARY

2. In paragraph A, what does the word *miniature* mean?

a. very beautiful
b. very small
c. very important

DETAIL

3. Where do most organisms on Earth live?

a. in the sea
b. on land or in the soil
c. in the air

MAIN IDEA

4. Liittschwager and his team used the cube to _____ .

a. collect different species for further study
b. test the quality of the soil and water
c. count and photograph different organisms

INFERENCE

5. In paragraph C, why does Liittschwager call the organisms "little gems"?

a. He thinks they are valuable and precious.
b. They are very difficult for him to see.
c. The organisms look like small stones.

David Liittschwager found this tiny baby octopus (1.1 cm across) in his coral reef sample.

SHORT ANSWER

B. Write short answers for these questions. Use information from the reading passage and the photo captions.

1. What can plants help maintain for humans and animals?

_____

2. Why was it difficult for Liittschwager's team to identify the creatures at the coral reef?

_____

3. Where did Liittschwager find over a hundred species that can't be found anywhere else?

_____

Understanding Sequence (1)—Processes

When you sequence events, you put them in the order in which they occur. Sequencing is important for gaining a deeper understanding of the relationship between events in a process. Some common words that can signal sequence are *first*, *after*, *then*, *later*, *next*, *once*, *when*, *as soon as*, and *finally*. A good way to show sequence is to list the events in a chain diagram.

IDENTIFYING **A.** Read paragraph B in Reading A again. Underline signal words that indicate a sequence.

SEQUENCING **B.** Put the life cycle events (a–f) in the correct order in the diagram below.

a. Plants and animals die.
b. Living plants get energy from the nutrients in the soil.
c. Plants help to support life for animals and humans.
d. Dead material is broken down.
e. Dead plants and animals fall to the ground.
f. Nutrients are returned to the soil.

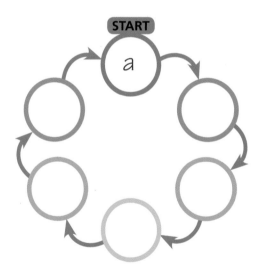

START
a

CRITICAL THINKING Applying Ideas Imagine you are a member of Liittschwager's team. In which of the environments below would you place a cube? Why? Check (✓) three options and discuss with a partner.

☐ a city park ☐ a riverbed ☐ a cave
☐ a treetop ☐ a backyard ☐ a mountain

⌄ **Liittschwager photographed hundreds of species living in this 3,200-year-old giant sequoia tree.**

VOCABULARY PRACTICE

COMPLETION   **A.** Circle the correct words to complete the information below.

One of the smallest animals in the world is a type of insect called a fairyfly. The male fairyfly of one [1]**species / team** is only 0.17 millimeters in length—about the size of the period at the end of this sentence. Not much is known about the life [2]**cycle / species** of fairyflies. But we do know they don't live long—only between 2 and 11 days.

Fairyflies live mostly in rain forests. The [3]**processes / regions** with the greatest number of species are in Australia, New Zealand, and South America. Recently, [4]**materials / scientists** in Costa Rica [5]**discovered / maintained** a new species of fairyfly called *Tinkerbella nana*.

∧ **The fairyfly is one of the world's smallest animals.**

WORDS IN CONTEXT   **B.** Complete each sentence with the correct answer (a or b).

1. A **process** refers to a _____.
   a. series of events   b. single event

2. If you **maintain** a healthy weight, it _____.
   a. changes often   b. doesn't change much

3. A **team** refers to _____.
   a. just one person   b. a group of people

4. Plant **material** would include _____.
   a. rocks and stones   b. grass and leaves

5. If you **break** something **down**, you _____.
   a. separate it into smaller pieces   b. give it away

COLLOCATIONS   **C. Break down** is one of many phrasal verbs formed using the verb *break*. Complete the definitions below using the prepositions in the box.

into	out of	up with

1. If you break _____ your boyfriend or girlfriend, your relationship with that person ends.

2. If a prisoner breaks _____ prison, they escape from it.

3. If someone breaks _____ a building, they enter it by force.

BEFORE YOU READ

DISCUSSION

A. Read this information. Then answer the questions below.

To learn about something (e.g., an animal or a plant), scientists must collect a lot of data. This can take a very long time. But now, regular people are helping scientists get important information more quickly. These "citizen scientists" take photos or interview other people. They then share their pictures and information with scientists on the Internet. Today, there are hundreds of citizen science projects—and anyone can join!

1. Who can be a citizen scientist?

2. What does a citizen scientist do? Why is this work important?

SKIMMING

Review this reading skill in Unit 1A

B. Read the introduction and the interview questions on the next page. Check (✓) the topics you think Gabby Salazar will discuss. Then read the interview to check your answers.

☐ a. different citizen science projects

☐ b. the problems with citizen science

☐ c. how to be a citizen scientist

National Geographic Explorer Gabby Salazar found this beautiful luna moth near her home in Pennsylvania, U.S.A.

WHAT'S IN YOUR NEIGHBORHOOD?

*Gabby Salazar takes photographs of **rare** species and teaches people about them. In this interview, she answers questions about her **experience** with citizen science.*

What was your first citizen science project?

A **Gabby Salazar:** It was over 10 years ago. One of my friends in Peru was very interested in birds. So we walked around with our cameras and notebooks for a day. We saw many different species, and we took photos of them. Later, we **posted** all our data on eBird.

What is eBird?

B **Gabby Salazar:** It's an Internet-based citizen science project at Cornell University in the United States. People around the world record information about birds they see. Today, eBird has over 590 million observations of more than 10,000 different bird species. Scientists use this data to answer important questions. For example: Where do certain birds live? How many are there?

How can a person become a citizen scientist?

C **Gabby Salazar:** It's easy. First, find a project that you like **online**. One of my favorites is iNaturalist, which studies animals and plants. Then, download the project's app[1] and use your phone to take pictures. For example, you can photograph different kinds of trees near your home or school. When you're done, **upload** your photos to iNaturalist. If you don't know the name of an animal or plant, other people can tell you. It's a great way to learn about your environment, and you also assist scientists with their **research**.

D If you can't take photos, you can still **contribute** to citizen science. For example, you can **take part** in a fun project called Wildwatch Kenya. Experts hide cameras in trees and other places. When an animal moves past, the camera takes a photo. Citizen scientists then **review** the **images** online and identify the animals they see.

THE LOST LADYBUG PROJECT

For years, scientists in North America thought the nine-spotted ladybug (pictured below) was extinct.[2] Then citizen scientist Peter Priolo photographed the insect in New York. He sent his photo to the Lost Ladybug Project, a site that is creating a map of different ladybug species. Now scientists know something important: The nine-spotted ladybug is rare, but not extinct.

---

1 An **app** (**application**) is a computer program for your phone or tablet.

2 If a species of animal or plant is **extinct**, it no longer exists.

A. Choose the best answer for each question.

PURPOSE

1. What is the purpose of this reading?

   a. to encourage people to take more photographs

   b. to describe somebody's experience with citizen science

   c. to answer important questions about certain bird species

DETAIL

2. Which of these statements about Gabby Salazar is NOT mentioned in the reading?

   a. She is a nature photographer.

   b. She is a citizen scientist.

   c. She is a motivational speaker.

REFERENCE

3. In the last sentence of paragraph D, what does *they* refer to?

   a. citizen scientists

   b. images

   c. animals

DETAIL

4. What did Peter Priolo send to the Lost Ladybug Project?

   a. an insect

   b. a photograph

   c. a map

INFERENCE

5. The nine-spotted ladybug _____ seen in New York.

   a. has never been

   b. can sometimes be

   c. is often

^ **Salazar with a carnivorous pitcher plant, Mount Kinabalu, Malaysia**

EVALUATING STATEMENTS

B. Are the following statements true or false according to the reading passage, or is the information not given? Circle T (true), F (false), or NG (not given).

1. Salazar first became involved in citizen science through iNaturalist.　T　F　NG

2. More than 590 million bird observations have been uploaded to eBird.　T　F　NG

3. Salazar is paid for the photos that she posts online.　T　F　NG

4. To take part in the Wildwatch Kenya project, people need to travel to Africa.　T　F　NG

5. Salazar has won awards for her work.　T　F　NG

Understanding Sequence (2)—Instructions or Directions

Previously, you learned about signal words for a sequence of events (see Unit 6A Reading Skill). These signal words can also help you understand a sequence of steps for how to do something, or directions for how to get to a particular place. For example, notice the signal words in these instructions for how to photograph a sunset:

First, get out there early to give yourself time to look around and find the best spot. **Next**, set up your camera. Try experimenting with different settings. **After** you have adjusted the settings, wait for the perfect moment and **then** take as many photos as you want. **Later**, you can develop the film or print out the pictures.

SEQUENCING **A.** Reading B describes how to become a citizen scientist. Look back at paragraph C and number these steps in the correct order (1–4).

- a. ____ Take a photograph using your phone.
- b. ____ Upload the photo using the app.
- c. ____ Download the app to your phone.
- d. ____ Find an interesting citizen science project online.

COMPLETION **B.** Read about how to take part in a citizen science project called NestWatch. Then complete the notes with words from the paragraph.

NestWatch is a program in which people can watch and report on bird nesting sites. It's easy to get started. First, visit the website to take a short test. If you pass, you become a certified "NestWatcher." Next, read the website's tips on how to find a nest in your area. After you find a nest, visit it every three or four days and keep a record of what you see. Then upload your observations to the website. Researchers will use this information to track bird populations and how their nesting sites change over time.

How to Become a NestWatcher

1. Take a short test on the organization's ¹_____.
2. Read the ²_____ on the website for finding bird nests.
3. Find a ³_____ in your area and ⁴_____ it every 3–4 days.
4. Record your observations and ⁵_____ them to the website.

CRITICAL THINKING Analyzing Information   Find a citizen science project online. Note the following information about it and then describe the project to a partner.

Project name: _____

Purpose: _____

How you can take part: _____

Unit 6B **87**

COMPLETION **A.** Complete the information with words from the box.

contribute	images	research	review	upload

Pl@ntNet is a citizen science project and an app that helps people identify plants using just their smartphones. It was developed by scientists from four French ¹_____ organizations. Users who know a lot about plants add photos and information to the database. Then, if someone wants to learn the name of a plant they see, they can download the app, take a photo of the plant, and ²_____ their photo to the database. The app will look for other plants in the database that look the same, and list the results. Finally, that user will need to ³_____ the results and confirm that their plant is one of the species from the list.

Currently, there are over 700,000 ⁴_____ in Pl@ntNet, and this number will continue to grow. "I think that users are quite proud to ⁵_____ to such a new collective knowledge," says Alexis Joly, one of the app's developers.

∧ **An Alice sundew flower**

WORDS IN CONTEXT **B.** Complete each sentence with the correct answer (a or b).

1. When you **post** information on the Internet, you _____.
   a. check it for accuracy
   b. make it available to other people

2. If you **take part** in an activity, you _____.
   a. finish or complete it
   b. do it together with other people

3. Something that is **rare** is _____.
   a. found in large numbers
   b. very unusual

4. If you have **experience** with a particular website, you _____ used it before.
   a. have
   b. have not

5. If you are **online**, your computer _____ connected to the Internet.
   a. is
   b. is not

COLLOCATIONS **C.** **Take part** is one of many collocations with the verb *take*. Complete the sentences using the words or phrases in the box. One option is extra.

a break	a photo	care	place

1. The conference will take _____ in October.

2. It is everyone's responsibility to take _____ of the environment.

3. The students had been studying for six hours, so they decided to take _____.

> A young volunteer studies insects at a BioBlitz event in Hawai'i Volcanoes National Park.

BIOBLITZ

BEFORE YOU WATCH

PREVIEWING **A.** Read the information. The words in **bold** appear in the video. Match these words with their definitions below.

A BioBlitz is a citizen science event that focuses on finding and **classifying** as many species as possible in a specific area over one or two days. It brings together scientists and other **volunteers**, and it can take place anywhere—from a large national park to a small schoolyard. The goal is to create an **inventory** of all the species that live in an area, and to show that nature is all around us. In 2014, the National Geographic Society helped organize a BioBlitz in the Golden Gate National Recreation Area in the United States. Volunteers found a great **diversity** of plants and animals there, including freshwater sponges, rare butterflies and snakes, and even a mountain lion.

1. classify •   • a. someone who does work without being paid for it
2. volunteer •   • b. the state of being different or varied
3. inventory •   • c. to put things into groups according to type
4. diversity •   • d. a complete list of all the things that are in a place

DISCUSSION **B.** What are some problems that people might face during a BioBlitz event? Would you be interested in taking part in one? Discuss with a partner.

SEQUENCING **A.** Read the sentences below. Then watch the video and number these actions from the BioBlitz event in the order you see them (1–5).

    a. ___ The volunteers work in the rain.

    b. _2_ A group of people catch and identify animals from a river.

    c. ___ The team leader announces how many species they found in the area.

    d. ___ The volunteers use a white sheet to see animals in the dark.

    e. ___ A young girl takes a close look at a frog.

MULTIPLE CHOICE **B.** Watch the video again. Choose the correct answer for each question.

    1. In the video, what does John Francis say happens "in some cases"?

      a. The BioBlitz takes longer than two days.

      b. The team finds new species in the area.

    2. What does John Johnson probably mean when he says, "Oh, nothing could be better"?

      a. Some animals prefer to come out in rainy weather.

      b. Even though it's raining, he's having a lot of fun exploring the area.

    3. What is the purpose of the festival that is held after the BioBlitz?

      a. to educate local people about the species in the area

      b. to encourage people to sign up for the next BioBlitz event

    4. How many species were discovered in this BioBlitz?

      a. almost 2,000   b. over 2,000

CRITICAL THINKING Applying Ideas Imagine you want to start your own citizen science project. What would it focus on? Note your ideas below and describe the project to a partner.

Project name: _____

Purpose: _____

How to take part: _____

_____

VOCABULARY REVIEW

Do you remember the meanings of these words? Check (✓) the ones you know. Look back at the unit and review any words you're not sure of.

Reading A

☐ break down   ☐ cycle*   ☐ discover   ☐ maintain*   ☐ material

☐ process*   ☐ region*   ☐ scientist   ☐ species   ☐ team*

Reading B

☐ contribute*   ☐ experience   ☐ image*   ☐ online   ☐ post

☐ rare   ☐ research*   ☐ review   ☐ take part   ☐ upload

* Academic Word List

7

WHEN DINOSAURS RULED

A dinosaur hunts sea reptiles in a scene from the Triassic Period.

WARM UP

Discuss these questions with a partner.

1. What movies about dinosaurs have you seen? Did you like them? Why or why not?

2. Why do you think people are interested in dinosaurs?

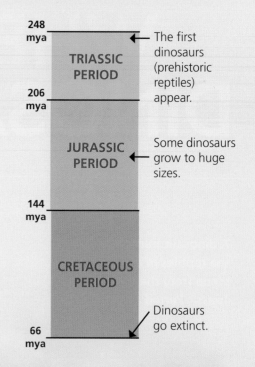

248 mya

TRIASSIC PERIOD

← The first dinosaurs (prehistoric reptiles) appear.

206 mya

JURASSIC PERIOD

Some dinosaurs grow to huge sizes.

144 mya

CRETACEOUS PERIOD

Dinosaurs go extinct.

66 mya

mya = million years ago

BEFORE YOU READ

DISCUSSION **A.** Look at the timeline on the right. Then answer the questions below.

 1. What kind of animals were dinosaurs?

 2. When did dinosaurs become extinct? What does *extinct* mean?

PREDICTING **B.** Read the three question headings on the next two pages. What do you think the answer is for each question? Check your ideas as you read the passage.

> *Tyrannosaurus rex* (*T. rex*) lived in the Late Cretaceous Period (about 68–66 million years ago).

THE **TRUTH** ABOUT DINOSAURS

A Dinosaurs are fascinating, but half-truths and myths about them are common. For years, scientists thought dinosaurs were just **giant** reptiles. Some dinosaurs *were* huge. But many were about the size of modern-day birds or dogs. Were dinosaurs warm- or cold-blooded? Paleontologists[1] are still not sure. But they now believe a few dinosaurs were intelligent. Some smaller ones—like the two-meter *Troodon*— had **fairly** large brains.

---

1 A **paleontologist** is a scientist who studies plants and animals that lived millions of years ago.

Was *T. rex* a powerful predator?

B While some scientists think *Tyrannosaurus rex* was a powerful predator, others think the **opposite** is true. For example, in the movies, *T. rex* is often a fast-moving giant. **In reality**, though, this dinosaur could not run fast. It was too large to move very quickly, so it **probably** moved about as fast as an elephant. *T. rex* also had very small arms and probably wasn't a powerful **hunter**. It may have been a scavenger instead, eating dead animals.

Could dinosaurs fly?

C Some reptiles, known as pterosaurs, were able to fly. But—even though they looked like them—these were not dinosaurs. Pterosaurs such as *Tupuxuara* could probably fly up to 16,000 kilometers nonstop. Scientists believe pterosaurs were actually very **heavy**. So they probably could not take off[2] from the ground like birds. Instead, they first had to drop or throw themselves from trees in order to fly—much like bats.

Are all dinosaurs extinct?

D Dinosaurs **completely** disappeared about 66 million years ago. Scientists think they died out because of a global **climate** change: The Earth's temperature became too cold for them to survive. Now you can only see dinosaurs in museums. However, scientists believe that modern-day birds are, in fact, dinosaurs' descendants. If this is true, then dinosaurs' **relatives** are still walking—and flying—among us!

---

2 If you **take off**, you leave the ground and start to fly.

⟨ *Tupuxuara*, a flying reptile, had wings that measured 5.5 meters from tip to tip.
When: 112–109 million years ago
Where: Brazil

READING COMPREHENSION

A. Choose the best answer for each question.

GIST

1. What could be another title for this reading?

   a. What Really Killed the Dinosaurs?
   b. Dinosaurs: Myths and Realities
   c. Dinosaurs' New Relatives

INFERENCE

2. Which statement about *Troodon* is probably true?

   a. It was the size of a small dog.
   b. It was warm-blooded.
   c. It was quite intelligent.

VOCABULARY

3. Some paleontologists think *T. rex* was a *scavenger* (paragraph B). What does this mean?

   a. It had small arms.
   b. It was a powerful killer.
   c. It ate dead or decaying material.

REFERENCE

4. What does *them* refer to in paragraph C, line 2?

   a. pterosaurs   b. dinosaurs   c. scientists

DETAIL

5. What happened 66 million years ago?

   a. Some dinosaurs started to fly.
   b. The first humans appeared on Earth.
   c. The last dinosaurs died out.

MATCHING **B.** Match each statement (1–5) with the creature it describes. Write a, b, or c.

   a. *Troodon*   b. *T. rex*   c. *Tupuxuara*

_____**1.** It could fly.

_____**2.** It had a large brain.

_____**3.** It was not very big.

_____**4.** It was too big to run fast.

_____**5.** It was a reptile but not a dinosaur.

Troodon >

Identifying Supporting Examples

Writers often use examples to support their ideas. This is important when claiming that something is true. Writers support a claim with examples—or *evidence*—so the reader is more likely to believe it. Examples can also help explain difficult ideas.

Words or phrases that signal examples include *for example, like,* and *such as*. Examples can also be shown in quotations, diagrams, and pictures.

NOTICING **A.** Circle the words or phrases in these sentences that signal examples.

1. Some smaller ones—like the two-meter *Troodon*—had fairly large brains.

2. For example, in the movies, *T. rex* is often a fast-moving giant.

3. Pterosaurs such as *Tupuxuara* could probably fly up to 16,000 kilometers nonstop.

IDENTIFYING **B.** Look again at sentences 1–3 above. Now underline the examples.

COMPLETION **C.** Complete each sentence with an example from the box (a–f). One example is extra.

a. *Brachiosaurus* weighed 80 tons	d. the *Jurassic World* series
b. grass and leaves	e. sharp points on their tails
c. *Stegosaurus*	f. jellyfish

1. Some dinosaurs, like _____, had brains the size of a walnut.

2. To defend themselves from predators, some plant-eating dinosaurs had natural protection, such as _____.

3. Some animals have been on Earth longer than dinosaurs. For example, _____ have existed for 650 million years.

4. Many dinosaurs were heavy. For example, _____. That's 17 African elephants!

5. There have been many movies about dinosaurs, such as _____.

CRITICAL THINKING Analyzing Theories

Scientists use words like *think, believe,* and *probably* to refer to theories—ideas that are based on evidence and reasoning but have not yet been proven.

▶ Underline three theories in Reading A and circle the signal word for each one.

▶ Do you agree with the theories you underlined? Discuss with a partner.

DEFINITIONS **A.** Read the information and match each word or phrase in **red** with its definition (1–5).

For centuries, stories about **giant** sea monsters have existed in many countries. One of the most famous is Scotland's Loch Ness Monster (often called "Nessie"). **In reality**, some animals that were like Nessie lived in the world's seas about 200 million years ago. Nessie looks like a type of plesiosaur—a sea reptile with a very long neck. But is Nessie really an ancient sea monster, still alive in a lake in Scotland? **Probably** not. Plesiosaurs (like the dinosaurs) died out **completely** about 66 million years ago, when the **climate** became cooler.

1. _____ : actually; in fact
2. _____ : huge; very large
3. _____ : totally
4. _____ : almost certainly
5. _____ : weather conditions over a long period of time

COMPLETION **B.** Circle the correct words to complete the paragraph below.

The ancient sea monster *Dakosaurus* is a [1]**reality / relative** of modern-day crocodiles. This large and [2]**heavy / fairly** South American sea reptile was a powerful [3]**climate / hunter**. Sea reptiles like *Dakosaurus* were dangerous predators. Some, such as *Tylosaurus*, even ate sharks. You might think that these fierce sea reptiles would have outlived sharks, but the [4]**fairly / opposite** is true. In the end, it was the sharks that survived.

▲ A *Dakosaurus* attacks a small *Plesiosaurus* in a prehistoric ocean.

WORD PARTS **C.** The suffixes *-er* and *-or* at the end of some verbs describe the person who does that action (e.g., *hunt* + *-er* = **hunter**). Add the correct suffixes to these verbs to complete the sentences. One verb is extra.

| act hunt invent teach |

1. If you have a question about your homework, ask your _____ .
2. My brother is studying drama. He wants to be a(n) _____ .
3. Thomas Edison was a famous _____ . He helped develop the modern light bulb.

New discoveries of dinosaur **fossils** have given us a better idea of what different dinosaurs looked like. Some had large **humps** on their backs, such as *Deinocheirus* (pictured). Others attacked their prey with **claws** like giant knives.

BEFORE YOU READ

DEFINITIONS **A.** Read the caption above. Match each word in **bold** with its definition (1–3).

1. _____ : the long, sharp nails on the toes or fingers of some animals

2. _____ : the bones or remains of an animal or plant

3. _____ : round raised parts on a person's or animal's back

PREDICTING **B.** Look at the picture of *Deinocheirus*. In what ways is this dinosaur unusual? Check your ideas as you read the passage.

The hand of *Deinocheirus*

MYSTERY
OF THE
TERRIBLE HAND

A *Whose hand is this?* For 50 years, paleontologists searched for an answer to this question. In 1965, paleontologists discovered a pair of giant arms in Ömnögovi, an area in Mongolia's Gobi Desert. The **length** of each arm was 2.4 meters. The claws were over 25 centimeters long. Paleontologists called the animal *Deinocheirus* (meaning "**terrible** hand").

B What did the body of this animal look like? Paleontologists had different **opinions**, but no one knew for sure. They **examined** the area many times, but found only a few other fossils of the dinosaur. So scientists used *Deinocheirus*'s arms to **estimate** its body size. Recently, however, a team of paleontologists **dug up** many more bones that tell us a lot about *Deinocheirus*'s appearance.

C *Deinocheirus* was one of the ornithomimosaurs—a type of dinosaur that looked like a modern-day ostrich.[1] It was 11 meters long and weighed 6,000 kilograms—almost as big as a *T. rex*! *Deinocheirus* was clearly very big, but it was not a predator. It couldn't move quickly, and, in fact, it had no teeth. Its head looked **similar** to a horse's head, and it had a long tail, **perhaps** with feathers at the end. Most surprisingly, though, *Deinocheirus* had a rounded hump or "sail" on its back. This dinosaur probably ate fish, small animals, and soft plants. Why did it need such long limbs?[2] Paleontologists now believe that its long arms were used simply to dig for food or to pull down high branches.

D So the **mystery** of the terrible hand, it seems, has been **solved**. It is amazing to see what *Deinocheirus* actually looked like and to find out more about this giant dinosaur. But Darla Zelenitsky from the University of Calgary says it's "also sad in a way." Even scientists like a bit of mystery, and "that mystery is now gone."

---

1 An **ostrich** is a very large bird that cannot fly.
2 Your **limbs** are your arms and legs.

A. Choose the best answer for each question.

PURPOSE

1. What is the main purpose of the reading?

a. to explain how paleontologists find dinosaur fossils

b. to compare *T. rex* and *Deinocheirus*

c. to describe an unusual type of dinosaur

INFERENCE

2. Why was *Deinocheirus* a mystery for so long?

a. No one knew who found the bones from the hands.

b. Paleontologists found only a few bones from the body.

c. Scientists could not agree on how long the arms were.

DETAIL

3. Which of these is true about *Deinocheirus*?

a. It was only a little smaller than a *T. rex*.

b. It had very sharp teeth.

c. Its body was the same shape as that of a horse.

DETAIL

4. According to the passage, what is the most unusual feature about *Deinocheirus*?

a. its head

b. its tail

c. its back

INFERENCE

5. Why does Darla Zelenitsky say it's "also sad in a way"?

a. *Deinocheirus* does not look the way she thought it would.

b. It was interesting to imagine what *Deinocheirus* looked like.

c. Someone else solved the mystery of *Deinocheirus*, not her.

MATCHING

B. Read the headings below. Match each one with a paragraph from the reading (A–D).

1. ___ Sometimes a Little Mystery Is a Good Thing

2. ___ In Search of More Bones

3. ___ A 50-Year-Old Mystery

4. ___ An Unusual-Looking Dinosaur

> This is what scientists used to think *Deinocheirus* looked like.

Finding Meaning (1)—Using Definitions

You will often find new words and phrases in a text. Some of these may be defined within the text. Certain words signal a definition, for example, *is, means, refers to*, and *is called*. Definitions can also be set off by certain punctuation: long dashes — , parentheses **( )** , commas **,** , or quotation marks **" "** . These may also signal extra information about people or places in the text.

Dinosaurs, which means **"terrible lizards,"** *lived millions of years ago.*

Ostriches—large flightless birds—live in Africa.

Nessie looks like a type of plesiosaur, *a sea reptile with a very long neck.*

COMPLETION **A. Complete the sentences with definitions from the box (a–d).**

⌄ **The skull of**
Cryolophosaurus

> a. the length of time it lived
> b. the world's most complete *T. rex* skeleton
> c. "tyrant lizard"
> d. (a growth of skin on the top of its head)

1. *Tyrannosaurus* means _____ in Greek. *Rex* means "king" in Latin.

2. A *T. rex*'s lifespan—_____—was about 30 years.

3. *Tyrannosaurus Sue*, _____, was found by fossil hunter Sue Hendrickson in 1990.

4. The dinosaur *Cryolophosaurus* is also known as "Elvisaurus." Fossils show that it had a head crest _____ that looked like Elvis Presley's 1950s hairstyle.

SCANNING **B. Use definitions in Reading B to answer these questions.**

1. What is Ömnögovi?

_____

2. What does the name *Deinocheirus* mean?

_____

3. What were ornithomimosaurs?

_____

CRITICAL THINKING Speculating **What do you think was the purpose of *Deinocheirus*'s hump on its back? Discuss with a partner and note some ideas.**

_____

_____

COMPLETION   **A.**   Complete the paragraph with words from the box.

estimate	length	perhaps	similar

The largest ever flying animal lived 71 million years ago. It was a type of pterosaur with a wingspan of 12 meters. That is the ¹_____ of some airplanes! Recently, a much smaller species of pterosaur was discovered in England. Paleontologists ²_____ that this creature (pictured) had a wingspan of about 75 centimeters and was ³_____ in size to a crow. It probably lived about 124 million years ago. What caused the change in body size? ⁴_____ competition between these flying reptiles led them to develop larger body sizes.

WORDS IN CONTEXT   **B.**   Complete each sentence with the correct answer (a or b).

1. If you **examine** something, you _____.
    a. look at it quickly   b. study it closely

2. A **mystery** is something you _____ explain.
    a. can   b. cannot

3. An example of an **opinion** is _____.
    a. "Dinosaurs were reptiles"   b. "Dinosaurs are very interesting"

4. If something is **terrible**, it makes you feel _____.
    a. bad or afraid   b. happy or relaxed

5. You **dig up** something that is _____ the surface.
    a. above   b. below

6. When you **solve** a problem or a question, you _____ an answer to it.
    a. find   b. don't find

COLLOCATIONS   **C.**   The words in the box are often used with the word **opinion**. Complete the sentences with the correct words from the box. One option is extra.

ask for	different	express	popular

1. "I'm sorry you didn't like what I said, but you did _____ my opinion."

2. "Please feel free to _____ your opinion. I want to hear your ideas."

3. "That's an interesting idea, but I actually have a(n) _____ opinion."

A dinosaur display at the
Children's Museum of
Indianapolis, Indiana

DINOSAURS:
A BRIEF HISTORY

BEFORE YOU WATCH

PREVIEWING **A. Read the information. The words in bold appear in the video. Circle the correct words to complete the definitions (1–3).**

Millions of people visit museums every year to see dinosaurs. It is fun to imagine what these creatures were like. Were they gentle **herbivores** or fierce **carnivores**? Did they live on their own or in social groups? Why did they become extinct? According to one theory, dinosaurs were killed by an **asteroid** that crashed into Earth. Other scientists believe that the main cause was a change in the world's climate. For now, at least, the case of the dinosaur killer remains an unsolved mystery.

1. A **herbivore** is an animal that eats only *other animals / plants*.

2. A **carnivore** is an animal that eats only *other animals / plants*.

3. An **asteroid** is *a type of star / a rock that travels through space*.

PREDICTING **B. Read the paragraph above again and the video title. Then look at the topics below. Check (✓) the topics you think will be covered in the video.**

☐ a. what dinosaurs ate

☐ b. how to identify dinosaur bones

☐ c. how dinosaurs lived in groups

☐ d. why dinosaurs died out

WHILE YOU WATCH

GIST **A.** Watch the video. Check your predictions in Before You Watch B.

MULTIPLE CHOICE **B.** Watch the video again. Choose the correct answer for each question.

1. Which of these statements about dinosaurs is true?

   a. They lived on a supercontinent that broke apart a long time ago.
   b. They traveled to different continents to lay eggs.

2. Which dinosaur species was particularly large?

   a. *Compsognathus*   b. *Dreadnoughtus*

3. According to the video, about 40 percent of dinosaurs were _____.

   a. herbivores   b. carnivores

4. Which statement better describes the narrator's opinion about why dinosaurs went extinct?

   a. They were all killed by an asteroid strike.
   b. They died out because of many reasons, including an asteroid strike.

CRITICAL THINKING Reflecting

▶ Think of the dinosaurs you learned about in this unit. If scientists could bring back one dinosaur species, which would you choose and why? Note your answer and reasons below.

_____

_____

▶ Do you think it's a good idea to bring back dinosaurs? Why or why not? Discuss with a partner.

VOCABULARY REVIEW

Do you remember the meanings of these words? Check (✓) the ones you know. Look back at the unit and review any words you're not sure of.

Reading A

☐ climate   ☐ completely   ☐ fairly   ☐ giant   ☐ heavy

☐ hunter   ☐ in reality   ☐ opposite   ☐ probably   ☐ relative

Reading B

☐ dig up   ☐ estimate*   ☐ examine   ☐ length   ☐ mystery

☐ opinion   ☐ perhaps   ☐ similar*   ☐ solve   ☐ terrible

* Academic Word List

STORIES AND STORYTELLERS

8

A scene from *Red Riding Hood*, a 2011 movie adaptation of the classic fairy tale

WARM UP

Discuss these questions with a partner.

1. What is one of your favorite books or stories? Why do you like it?

2. Can you think of a very old story that is still popular today? Why do you think it is still popular?

DISCUSSION **A.** Skim the reading quickly. What kind of stories did the Grimm brothers write? Who were their stories for? Read the passage to check your ideas.

THE BROTHERS GRIMM

A   Jacob and Wilhelm Grimm were two young men from Germany who loved reading stories. As university students, they became interested in folktales—traditional stories or legends that people told again and again, often for generations. The brothers began to **collect** folktales from storytellers all over Germany. Many were similar to stories told in France, Italy, Japan, and other countries. Between 1812 and 1814, the brothers **published** two books in German. These included stories like "Cinderella," "Snow White," and "Little Red Riding Hood." The collections became known in English as *Grimms' Fairy Tales*.

Darkness and Magic

B   The Grimm brothers' tales give a picture of traditional life and **beliefs**. For example, in the past, many people in Germany believed that forests were dangerous places. In the Grimms' stories, a forest is often the home of evil witches (as in "Hansel and Gretel"), talking animals, and other **magical** beings.

Children's Stories?

C   **Although** most people today think of these stories as fairy tales for children, the Grimm brothers first wrote them **primarily** for adults. Many of their early tales were dark and **scary**. Later, the brothers changed the **text** of some of the original stories. They "softened" many of the tales and **added** drawings. This made them more **suitable** for children. Like the early tales, though, each story still has a moral: Work hard, be good, and listen to your parents.

A. Choose the best answer for each question.

PURPOSE

1. What is the main purpose of the reading?

    a. to compare the Grimms' stories with modern children's stories

    b. to explain why storytelling is important in Germany

    c. to give information about the Grimm brothers and their stories

REFERENCE

2. What does *Many* refer to in paragraph A?

    a. folktales

    b. storytellers

    c. books

DETAIL

3. Which of these is true about the Grimm brothers?

    a. They invented the fairy tales in their books.

    b. They became interested in folktales as students.

    c. They wrote their books in different languages.

VOCABULARY

4. In paragraph C, what does *moral* mean?

    a. interest   b. story   c. message

DETAIL

5. Which of these is true about the Grimms' stories?

    a. The early stories were written mainly for children.

    b. Both the early stories and the later versions contained morals.

    c. The early stories had a lot of drawings.

△ **The Grimm brothers have inspired many movies, some of which have been translated into different languages.**

IDENTIFYING SUPPORTING EXAMPLES

Review this reading skill in Unit 7A

B. Write short answers for these questions. Use information from the reading passage.

1. What is the title of a story that the Grimm brothers published in German?

_____

2. What example is given of a story that includes an evil witch?

_____

3. List one way the Grimm brothers made their stories more suitable for children.

_____

4. What is an example of a moral that appears in Grimms' fairy tales?

_____

Annotating Text (1)

As you read a passage in detail, it may be useful to mark—or annotate—the text. This allows you to focus on the most important information, and to remember it later. Here are some ways to add annotations.

- Use one or more colors to highlight the main ideas or most important parts.
- Underline new words and write their definitions in the margins.
- Put a circle around important numbers, statistics, or dates.
- Put a question mark (?) next to things you don't understand, for checking later.

ANNOTATING **A.** Look at the annotated paragraph below from "The Brothers Grimm." Then annotate the rest of Reading A.

Jacob and Wilhelm Grimm were two young men from Germany who loved reading stories. As university students, they became interested in folktales—traditional stories or legends that people told again and again, often for generations. The brothers began

people who write or tell stories ← to collect folktales from storytellers all over Germany. Many were similar to stories told in France, Italy, Japan, and other countries. Between 1812 and 1814, the brothers published two books in German. These included stories like "Cinderella," "Snow White," and "Little Red Riding Hood." The collections became known in English as *Grimms' Fairy Tales*.

SUMMARIZING **B.** Look back at your annotated text in Reading A. Then complete the concept map below with words from the reading.

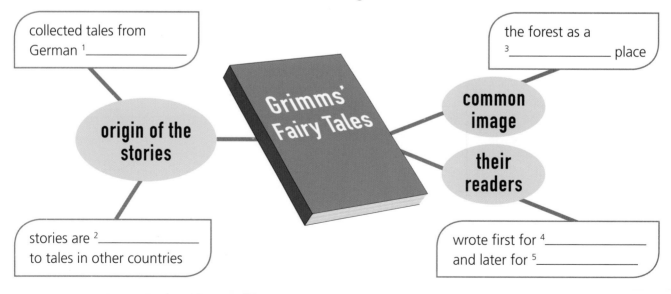

collected tales from German ¹_____

the forest as a ³_____ place

origin of the stories

Grimms' Fairy Tales

common image

their readers

stories are ²_____ to tales in other countries

wrote first for ⁴_____ and later for ⁵_____

CRITICAL THINKING Analyzing Stories   Discuss with a partner. Can you think of any recent movies or TV shows based on traditional stories or legends? What changes were made (e.g., to the story, characters, or moral)? Why do you think these changes were made?

COMPLETION **A.** Circle the correct words to complete the information below.

In Finland, there was once an area known as Viena Karelia. The people there were great storytellers and had many folktales and legends. The most famous of these is the *Kalevala*. This is a ¹**collection** / **text** of several poems that forms one long story. The *Kalevala* tells tales of ²**magical** / **suitable** beings and ³**suitable** / **scary** monsters.

For centuries, storytellers—called *rune singers*—learned and spoke the *Kalevala* from memory. Jussi Huovinen (1924–2017) was Finland's last great rune singer. When he died, the ancient culture of singing the *Kalevala* came to an end.

⁴**Primarily** / **Although** Jussi Huovinen was the last rune singer, many of the Finnish and Karelian folk ⁵**beliefs** / **additions** from the *Kalevala* still live on today. British author J.R.R. Tolkien included many of the *Kalevala*'s ideas in stories he wrote about a fantasy land called Middle-earth. First ⁶**published** / **added** in 1954, Tolkien's *The Lord of the Rings* has since become one of the best-selling books of all time.

△ **Arwen (a character from *The Lord of the Rings*) in the movie adaptation**

DEFINITIONS **B.** Match the words in **red** in activity A with these definitions (1–7).

1. _____ : the words in a written work

2. _____ : for the most part; mainly

3. _____ : put in; included

4. _____ : having special powers

5. _____ : right or acceptable for a particular person or situation

6. _____ : ideas a person accepts as being true or real

7. _____ : printed (as a book for sale)

WORD FORMS **C.** We can add *-al* to some nouns to form adjectives (e.g., *magic* + *-al* = **magical**). Complete the sentences using the nouns in the box. One noun is extra.

magic	music	nation	origin

1. In addition to rune singing, Jussi Huovinen also played _____**al** instruments such as the fiddle and the accordion.

2. In the fairy tale "Jack and the Beanstalk," Jack trades his cow for beans he believes are _____**al**.

3. The _____**al** story of "Little Red Riding Hood" can be traced back to 10th-century France.

BEFORE YOU READ

DISCUSSION   **A.** "The Seven Ravens" is a fairy tale collected by the Brothers Grimm. Read paragraph A. Then answer these questions.

     1. How many children did the couple have?

     2. Why were the brothers in the forest?

     3. What happened there?

PREDICTING   **B.** What do you think happens next in the story? Discuss with a partner. Then read the rest of the story to find out.

THE SEVEN RAVENS

A Once upon a time, there lived a man and a woman who had seven sons. The couple wanted a daughter, and, eventually, they had a girl who they loved very much. One day, the father needed water for the child, so he sent the seven brothers to a well in the forest to get it. Once there, though, the boys began to fight, and the water jug fell into the well. The boys did not know what to do. They were **afraid** to go home.

B Hours passed. "Where are those boys?" shouted the **angry** father. "They are probably playing a game and **forgot** about the water. I wish they were all turned into ravens!" When he looked up, he saw seven black birds flying away. The father was **shocked**. "What have I done?" he thought. But it was too late. He could not take back his words.

C In time, the girl grew up and discovered she had brothers. The story of their misfortune[1] **affected** her greatly, and she was **determined** to find them. For years, she searched and did not stop. Finally, she found their home. To enter, she needed a special key made from a chicken bone, which she did not have. The girl thought for a **moment**, and then took a knife and cut off one of her fingers. With it, she opened the front door and went inside. On a table, there were seven plates and seven cups. She ate and drank a little from each of them. In the last cup, she accidentally[2] dropped a ring that her parents had given her.

D Eventually, the ravens returned for their meal. The girl hid behind a door and watched. When the seventh raven drank from his cup, something hit his mouth. The raven **recognized** it **immediately**—it was his parents' ring. "I wish our sister were here," he said, "and then we could be free." Their sister quickly ran to them, and **suddenly** the ravens were human again. The brothers kissed their sister, and they all went home together happily.

---

1 **Misfortune** is bad luck.
2 If something happens **accidentally**, it happens without you planning it.

A. Choose the best answer for each question.

GIST

1. What is this story mainly about?

    a. a father who leaves his children

    b. a sister who saves her brothers

    c. magical birds that help children

VOCABULARY

2. In paragraph B, what does *turned into* mean?

    a. changed to

    b. returned to

    c. circled around

PARAPHRASE

3. What does *He could not take back his words* (paragraph B) mean?

    a. He could not remember what he had said.

    b. He had already said the words, so it was too late.

    c. He could not think of the right thing to say.

DETAIL

4. Why does the girl cut off her finger?

    a. because her finger is trapped in a door

    b. because she needs it to change the ravens back into humans

    c. so she can use it to enter the ravens' house

INFERENCE

5. What lesson or moral is taught in this story?

    a. Your parents know what is best for you.

    b. Think carefully about what you say.

    c. Work hard and you will be happy.

∧ A *kitsune* (fox) mask from Japan. In Japanese folktales, clever fox spirits can turn into beautiful women.

SEQUENCING

Review this reading skill in Unit 6A

B. Number these events in the correct order (1–8) to summarize paragraphs C and D. Then practice retelling the story to a partner.

a. _____ The girl found the boys' home.

b. _____ One raven made a wish.

c. __1__ The girl learned that she had brothers.

d. _____ The girl went inside the house.

e. _____ The girl ran to her brothers.

f. _____ The girl dropped a ring into a cup.

g. _____ The girl cut off one of her fingers.

h. _____ The ravens came home to eat.

Understanding Pronoun Reference

Pronouns are words such as *he*, *she*, *they*, and *them*, and usually refer to a noun earlier in a text. Writers use pronouns when they don't want to repeat the same names or words over and over again. To fully understand a text, it is important to know what each pronoun refers to. Notice that pronouns usually match the gender and number of the noun.

The father needed water. He sent the brothers to a well to get it. Once there, they began to fight.

MATCHING **A.** Read this summary of the fairy tale "Hansel and Gretel." Then draw an arrow to the word or phrase each underlined pronoun refers to.

Once upon a time, there were two children named Hansel and Gretel. Their mother had died when ¹they were young. Their father married again—to a terrible woman who became their stepmother. One day, ²she took the children deep into the forest and left ³them there.

After walking for a long time, Hansel and Gretel saw a house made of chocolate, candy, and cake. They broke off a piece of ⁴it and started to eat. An old woman opened the door and let them in. ⁵She gave them food and let them stay in the house. But this old woman was a witch. ⁶She wanted to make the children fatter so that she could cook and eat ⁷them!

One day, Hansel and Gretel escaped. They pushed the witch into the oven and shut ⁸it. When they reached home, they learned that their stepmother had died. Hansel and Gretel stayed with their father, and all three of them lived happily ever after.

REFERENCE **B.** Find these sentences in Reading B. Write the word or phrase each underlined pronoun refers to.

1. With it, she opened the front door and went inside. (paragraph C) _____

2. She ate and drank a little from each of them. (paragraph C) _____

3. …, and they all went home together happily. (paragraph D) _____

CRITICAL THINKING Applying Ideas   Imagine you are turning "The Seven Ravens" into a movie for children. What changes would you make to the story? Would you "soften" it in any way? Discuss with a partner and note your ideas.

WORDS IN
CONTEXT

A. Complete each sentence with the correct answer (a or b).

1. You feel **angry** when you think someone has behaved _____ .

   a. badly   b. well

2. If something happens **immediately** or **suddenly**, it happens _____ .

   a. repeatedly   b. quickly

3. A **moment** refers to a very _____ period of time.

   a. short   b. long

4. You **recognize** a person or thing you _____ .

   a. know   b. don't know

5. If you are **shocked** by something, it surprises you—usually in a _____ way.

   a. good   b. bad

6. If you are **afraid** to do something, you are _____ .

   a. scared of what might happen   b. looking forward to it

COMPLETION

B. Complete the paragraph with words from the box.

affect	determined	forget

Sol Guy and Josh Thome are modern-day storytellers. Through their TV show, *4REAL*, they share real-life fairy tales about young people who are ¹_____ to make a difference and improve lives. Each *4REAL* show takes a celebrity to a different country. There, they meet young leaders who are helping other people in their community (e.g., by building community centers or by providing medical care). Guy and Thome hope that the stories will ²_____ viewers in ways they won't ³_____, and raise public awareness of social issues around the world.

∧ **Thome and Guy have worked
with celebrities including actress
Cameron Diaz (pictured here).**

WORD USAGE

C. The word **affect** (verb) is often confused with *effect* (noun). Circle the correct word to complete each sentence.

1. The earthquake *affected / effected* thousands of people.

2. What *affect / effect* does reading stories to children have on their development?

3. The movie did not *affect / effect* me as much as I thought it would.

FAIRY-TALE
CASTLE

> **Mist surrounds Neuschwanstein Castle in the Bavarian Alps, Germany.**

BEFORE YOU WATCH

PREVIEWING

A. Read the information. The words in **bold** appear in the video. Match these words with their definitions below.

High on a hilltop in Germany sits one of the most famous castles in Europe: Neuschwanstein Castle. It was built by King Ludwig II of Bavaria (1845–1886). As a boy, Ludwig II loved listening to **operas** by the German **composer** Richard Wagner. Many of Wagner's operas were based on legends of brave knights and noble ladies. Because of this, Ludwig II is sometimes called the "Swan King" (after Wagner's opera *Lohengrin* and its Swan Knight).

In 1869, King Ludwig began building Neuschwanstein Castle far away from his **court** in the city. Today, Neuschwanstein is one of the most popular tourist attractions in Europe. It has even been featured in several movies, including *The Wonderful World of the Brothers Grimm*.

1. opera • • a. a person who writes music, especially classical music

2. composer • • b. a play with music in which all or most of the words are sung

3. court • • c. the place where a king or queen lives and carries out their duties

WHILE YOU WATCH

MAIN IDEA **A.** Watch the video. Check (✓) the reasons Ludwig II built Neuschwanstein Castle.

☐ a. to have a place to relax away from public life

☐ b. to protect himself from enemies

☐ c. to honor the works of Richard Wagner

MULTIPLE CHOICE **B.** Watch the video again. Complete each sentence with the correct answer.

1. Neuschwanstein Castle is located _____ Ludwig II's childhood home.

a. near   b. far away from

2. According to the video, Ludwig II filled his castle with paintings of _____ .

a. Wagner and other composers   b. poets and kings

3. Neuschwanstein Castle was _____ .

a. completed after Ludwig II died   b. never completed

4. According to the video, Neuschwanstein was the inspiration for _____ .

a. Disneyland's Sleeping Beauty Castle

b. Hogwarts Castle in the Harry Potter series

CRITICAL THINKING Making Predictions   Many of the stories collected by the Grimm brothers are hundreds of years old but are still read by people today. Which stories (e.g., books, comics, movies) from the last 100 years do you think will still be popular hundreds of years from now? Why? Discuss with a partner and note your ideas.

_____

_____

_____

VOCABULARY REVIEW

Do you remember the meanings of these words? Check (✓) the ones you know. Look back at the unit and review any words you're not sure of.

Reading A

☐ add   ☐ although   ☐ belief   ☐ collect   ☐ magical

☐ primarily*   ☐ publish*   ☐ scary   ☐ suitable   ☐ text*

Reading B

☐ affect*   ☐ afraid   ☐ angry   ☐ determined   ☐ forget

☐ immediately ☐ moment   ☐ recognize   ☐ shocked   ☐ suddenly

* Academic Word List

UNUSUAL
JOBS

9

⌄ A golf ball diver collects balls from the bottom of a golf course pond.

WARM UP

Discuss these questions with a partner.

1. What are some unusual or challenging jobs? Make a list.

2. Would you like to do any of the jobs you've listed? Why or why not?

117

▲ A bright meteor streaks
past the star Sirius.

BEFORE YOU READ

DISCUSSION **A.** Read this brief description of meteorites. Then answer the questions with a partner.

Meteors are space rocks that travel through Earth's atmosphere, leaving streaks of light in the sky. Because of their appearance, they are sometimes called "shooting stars." If a piece of a meteor lands on Earth, it is called a meteorite. More than 50,000 meteorites have been found on Earth so far.

1. What is a meteorite?

2. Why do you think scientists are interested in meteorites? What can they learn from them?

SKIMMING **B.** Look quickly at the interview on the next two pages and answer these questions. Then read the interview to check your ideas.

1. What is Michael Farmer's job? What does he do, exactly?

2. What do you think are the challenging parts of his job?

MEET THE METEORITE HUNTER

Michael Farmer is a meteorite hunter. Here, he talks about his unusual job.

A **National Geographic (NG):** What's the hardest part of your job?

Michael Farmer: I'm always looking for new pieces [of meteorite rock], so I have to travel a lot. I've been to about 70 countries or so. The job can be dangerous because some rocks are **worth** a lot of money. On one such trip, I was robbed and almost killed. That was scary. There are other issues, too. It's **illegal** to take meteorite pieces from some countries. So you have to be very careful and learn the **law**. It's different everywhere.

B **NG:** Are there a lot of meteorite pieces on Earth?

Michael Farmer: Yes, there are millions, but most land in the forest, jungle, or ocean. They're almost impossible to **locate**. One of the best places to find pieces is in the Sahara Desert in Africa. You can see them easily in the sand. The heat also **preserves** the rocks well.

C **NG:** What's the most **valuable** meteorite you've found?

Michael Farmer: I found one piece in the Middle East, and I sold it for $100,000. It was a small piece—about the size of a walnut. But the most valuable was in Canada. Three partners and I discovered a very rare type of meteorite called a pallasite. It **weighed** 53 kilograms, and it's around 4.5 billion years old. We sold it to the Canadian government for just under a million dollars. Now it's in the Royal Ontario Museum in Toronto. It's a national **treasure**.

D **NG:** Who else buys the rocks from you?

Michael Farmer: Museums and private **collectors** are always calling me. New meteorites are **in demand**, and so they sell quickly. I also sell them to a lot of scientists. They don't have the time or money to search for these rocks. Without the help of hunters, 99 percent of these meteorites would be lost to science.

⌃ **This 2,200 kg iron-nickel meteorite was found in the Empty Quarter, Saudi Arabia.**

A. Choose the best answer for each question.

PURPOSE

1. What is the main purpose of this reading?

　a. to describe what a meteorite hunter does

　b. to explain why hunting for meteorites is challenging

　c. to give advice on how to become a meteorite hunter

DETAIL

2. What does Farmer say is difficult about his job?

　a. preserving meteorites

　b. traveling to find meteorites

　c. selling meteorites

DETAIL

3. Why is the Sahara Desert a good place to find meteorites?

　a. The sand makes it easy to spot meteorites.

　b. Most meteorites land there.

　c. The meteorites there are bigger than elsewhere.

DETAIL

4. Which of the following is true about the meteorite Farmer found in Canada?

　a. It is about the size of a walnut.

　b. It is more than four billion years old.

　c. Farmer found it by himself, without any help.

PARAPHRASE

5. In paragraph D, Farmer says, "New meteorites are in demand." What does he mean?

　a. New meteorites are easily available to collectors.

　b. New meteorites are very useful to collectors.

　c. New meteorites are popular among collectors.

⌃ **The 60-ton Hoba Meteorite in Namibia is the largest meteorite ever found.**

UNDERSTANDING PRONOUN REFERENCE

Review this reading skill in Unit 8B

B. Find these sentences in the reading. Write the word or phrase each underlined pronoun refers to.

1. <u>It</u>'s different everywhere. (paragraph A)　_____

2. You can see <u>them</u> easily in the sand. (paragraph B)　_____

3. <u>It</u>'s a national treasure. (paragraph C)　_____

4. …, and so <u>they</u> sell quickly. (paragraph D)　_____

5. <u>They</u> don't have the time or money to search for these rocks. (paragraph D)　_____

Identifying Exact vs. Approximate Numbers

Writers may use exact numbers (e.g., *at noon, a hundred years ago, 49 percent*) in a text if they are sure of the facts or if it is important to give a specific figure; they may also use approximate numbers (e.g., *around noon, almost a hundred years ago, nearly 50 percent*) if they aren't sure or if it is better to provide a larger range. These words indicate an approximate number: *about, around, approximately, nearly, almost, (just) under, (just) over, circa*, and *… or so*.

IDENTIFYING **A.** Read the following text. Circle the exact numbers. Underline the approximate numbers.

Only 200 or so meteorites from Mars have been found on Earth. One Martian meteorite was found in the Sahara Desert in 2011. Nicknamed "Black Beauty," the baseball-sized meteorite weighs just over 300 grams. At around 2.1 billion years old, it is the second-oldest Martian meteorite ever discovered on Earth.

After over a year of study, scientists found that Black Beauty contains approximately 10 times more water than other Martian meteorites. Scientists say this shows that Mars was warmer and wetter in the past than previously believed.

∧ **The Martian meteorite known as "Black Beauty"**

SHORT ANSWER **B.** Answer these questions about Reading A with exact or approximate numbers.

1. How many countries has Michael Farmer traveled to? _____

2. What was the selling price for the meteorite Farmer found in the Middle East? _____

3. How old is the pallasite that Farmer and his team found? _____

4. How much did the pallasite weigh? _____

CRITICAL THINKING Justifying an Opinion   Which of the following statements do you agree with? Why? Check (✓) the option that best reflects your opinion. Then discuss your reasons with a partner.

☐ Meteorite hunters should be allowed to sell meteorites to anyone, including private collectors.

☐ Meteorite hunters should only be allowed to sell meteorites to museums or scientists.

☐ Meteorites should not be sold at all; they should be left where they are found.

VOCABULARY PRACTICE

COMPLETION **A.** Complete the information with words or phrases from the box.

illegal	in demand	law	locate	valuable	worth

Good doctors and lawyers are always ¹_____, and so they often make good money. But what are some unusual jobs that also pay well?

A **hacker** is someone who can get into a computer system without permission. This is usually ²_____, but it is possible to be a hacker and not break the ³_____. Some companies give jobs to hackers because they can help identify problems with the company's computers and give ⁴_____ advice.

An **upcycler** changes trash into something more useful—something that may even be ⁵_____ a great deal of money. First, upcyclers need to ⁶_____ and gather items that people no longer need—like candy wrappers, or an old suitcase. Then they turn those items into things people might want to buy, like a bag or a coffee table.

∧ **An upcycled chair made of used skis**

WORDS IN CONTEXT **B.** Complete the sentences. Circle the correct words.

1. One way to **preserve** fruit is to *fry / freeze* it.

2. If someone **weighs** a suitcase, they find out how *heavy / tall* it is.

3. An example of **treasure** is *a set of gold coins / a can of paint*.

4. An art **collector** is someone who *makes / buys* rare or beautiful works of art.

COLLOCATIONS **C.** The words in the box are often used with the word **treasure**. Complete the sentences with the correct words from the box. One word is extra.

buried	chest	hunt	national

1. Archeologists found gold coins inside the treasure _____.

2. Stories about pirates often include a search for _____ treasure.

3. The panda is considered one of China's _____ treasures.

BEFORE YOU READ

DEFINITIONS **A.** Read the caption below. Match the correct form of each word in **bold** with its definition (1–3).

    1. _____ : to damage by fire

    2. _____ : an area of land that is 10,000 square meters

    3. _____ : a large fire that spreads quickly through a forest or over grassland

PREDICTING **B.** Read the introduction to the passage on the next page. What do you think smokejumpers do? How do they help to stop wildfires? Discuss with a partner. Then read the passage to check your ideas.

> Thousands of **wildfires** occur around the world every year. These fires **burn** millions of **hectares** of land.

SMOKEJUMPERS

Every year, wildfires destroy millions of hectares of forest land. Homes are damaged, and thousands of people die. Smokejumpers help to stop this.

A Smokejumpers are a special type of firefighter. They jump from planes or are lowered by helicopters into areas that are difficult to reach by car or on foot, such as the **middle** of a mountain forest. They **race** to put out fires as fast as they can.

B At a fire site, smokejumpers first examine the land and decide how to fight the fire. Their main goal is to stop a fire from spreading or to slow its progress until full, ground-based firefighters arrive. Using basic **equipment** such as shovels and axes,[1] smokejumpers clear land of burnable[2] material, like dry grass and dead trees. They carry water with them, too, but only a **limited** amount.

C Although the **majority** of smokejumpers are men, more women are joining now. The most important factors are your **height** and weight. Smokejumpers **employed** in the United States, for example, must be between 120 and 200 pounds (between 54 and 91 kilograms) so they don't get blown away by the strong winds or get hurt when they land. Smokejumpers must also be **capable** of surviving in the wilderness. In Russia, many smokejumpers know how to find food in the forest and can even make simple furniture[3] from trees.

D The work is dangerous, and the hours are long. But for these firefighters, smokejumping isn't just an **occupation**. They love being able to jump out of planes, fight fires, and live in the forest. As 28-year-old Russian smokejumper Alexi Tishin says, "This is the best job for tough guys."

---

1 A **shovel** is a tool used for digging earth; an **ax** is a tool used for cutting wood.
2 If something is **burnable**, it can start a fire easily.
3 Objects such as chairs, tables, and beds are referred to as **furniture**.

A. Choose the best answer for each question.

GIST   **1.** What is the reading mainly about?

a. the life of a Russian smokejumper

b. who smokejumpers are and what they do

c. why people become smokejumpers

DETAIL   **2.** When a smokejumper reaches a fire site, what is the first thing he or she does?

a. look for water

b. clear the land

c. study the land

DETAIL   **3.** If you want to be a smokejumper, you must be _____ .

a. within a certain weight range

b. male

c. a university graduate

DETAIL   **4.** Which of the following is NOT mentioned in the reading?

a. Smokejumpers put out fires in areas that are hard to reach.

b. Smokejumpers must learn to survive in the wilderness.

c. Smokejumpers are paid more than regular firefighters.

INFERENCE   **5.** In Alexi Tishin's opinion, why do people become smokejumpers?

a. for the money

b. for the excitement

c. to help their country

⌃ **A Russian smokejumper is lowered into a forest from a helicopter.**

SHORT ANSWER   **B. Write short answers for these questions. Use information from the reading passage.**

1. What are two types of equipment that a smokejumper uses?

_____

2. What does a smokejumper clear from the land?

_____

3. What is an example of an outdoor survival skill that a smokejumper needs?

_____

Annotating Text (2)

It is useful to annotate a text by highlighting key information, underlining new words and then defining them, and circling important numbers or statistics (see Unit 8A Reading Skill). Another way to annotate text is to note down the main idea of each paragraph in the margins, and then add any key points under these main ideas. This is especially useful when studying for an exam, as you can easily see the important details you noted down when you reread the passage.

MAIN IDEA **A.** Look at the main ideas below. Write each one next to the correct paragraph (A–D) in Reading B.

- How smokejumpers fight fires
- What a smokejumper is
- Why people like being smokejumpers
- Requirements to be a smokejumper

ANNOTATING **B.** Look back at Reading B and the main ideas you wrote in the margins. Add any key points below each main idea.

^ **Smokejumpers parachute from a plane.**

CRITICAL THINKING Ranking/Speculating

▶ Rank these jobs 1–7 (1 = most dangerous; 7 = least dangerous). Then compare answers with a partner.

_____ a circus performer

_____ a war journalist

_____ a private detective

_____ a window cleaner for a high-rise building

_____ a long-distance truck driver

_____ a commercial airline pilot

_____ a ski instructor

▶ Choose three of the jobs listed above. Why do you think people decide to take these jobs? Write reasons for each job and discuss with a partner.

1. Job: _____

Reason(s): _____

2. Job: _____

Reason(s): _____

3. Job: _____

Reason(s): _____

COMPLETION   **A.** Complete the information with words from the box.

> capable   employed   equipment   majority   occupation   race

As an 18-year-old student, A.J. Coston lived with his family during the week. But

on the weekends, Coston lived and worked at a fire station, where he was

¹_____ as a volunteer firefighter. Several times each weekend, he

had to ²_____ to the scene of a fire.

Firefighting is a dangerous ³_____. To get the job, Coston took classes

and learned safety skills. He also learned to use firefighting ⁴_____

such as axes and hoses. After Coston became ⁵_____ of using these well,

he was allowed to work inside burning buildings.

Although firefighters spend the ⁶_____ of their time putting out fires,

they also rescue people from accidents and other dangerous situations. Coston hopes

to be a flight paramedic in the future, but he will never forget his days as a firefighter.

WORDS IN   **B.** Complete each sentence with the correct answer (a or b).
CONTEXT

1. If something is **limited**, it is _____.

   a. in short supply   b. more than enough

2. If you **destroy** something, it can _____ be used again.

   a. now   b. never

3. We measure **height** in _____.

   a. kilograms   b. centimeters

4. If a book is in the **middle** of a table, it is _____ of the table.

   a. in the center   b. near the edge

WORD FORMS   **C.** We can add *-ment* to some verbs to form nouns (e.g., *equip* + *-ment* = **equipment**).
Complete the sentences using the verbs in the box. One verb is extra.

> **agree   employ   equip   improve**

1. The new smokejumper is getting better at his job, but there is still room for

_____**ment**.

2. Besides a shovel, what other _____**ment** does an archeologist need?

3. After graduating from college, she found _____**ment** at a local bank.

> ⌄ Mike Rochford (holding the snake's head) and his team caught this Burmese python in the Florida Everglades. It had recently eaten a 1.8-meter-long alligator.

SNAKE CATCHERS

BEFORE YOU WATCH

PREVIEWING **A.** Read the information. The words in **bold** appear in the video. Circle the correct words to complete the definitions (1–4).

Most of the time, scientists studying animals in the wild want to see them grow in number. However, the opposite is true for **invasive** species, like Burmese pythons in Florida. Burmese pythons are among the largest snakes on Earth, and are **native** to the rain forests of Southeast Asia. In the 1980s, these snakes were brought to Florida as pets. Later, however, many were dumped in the **swamps** by their owners. Since then, Burmese pythons have increased in numbers to tens of thousands, and have destroyed the populations of native wildlife. In the Everglades National Park in Florida, scientists Mike Rochford and Skip Snow are using special equipment such as **antennas** to catch these snakes and study their movements.

1. A species described as **invasive** *is / is not* originally from the local area, and is usually *harmful / helpful* to other animals.

2. If you are **native** to a place, you *often travel / were born* there.

3. A **swamp** is an area of very *wet and soft / dry and hard* land.

4. An **antenna** is a device that can *send and receive radio or television signals / turn radios and televisions on*.

WHILE YOU WATCH

COMPLETION **A.** **Read the notes below. Then watch the video and complete these notes.**

Invasive Burmese Pythons in the Florida Everglades

- eat native birds, small mammals, and large ¹_____
- capable of reaching ²_____m in length and weighing up to ³_____kg
- Everglades National Park area: ⁴_____ million acres

MULTIPLE CHOICE **B.** **Watch the video again. Choose the correct answer for each question.**

1. According to the video, how do Skip Snow and Mike Rochford track the pythons?
   a. by putting small tracking devices inside the snakes
   b. by tying radio collars around the snakes' bodies

2. Why does the team in the video use a plane?
   a. to move the pythons to another location
   b. to help look for the pythons

3. Which of these statements is true?
   a. The team managed to control the Everglades' population of Burmese pythons.
   b. The team is still trying to solve the Burmese python problem in the Everglades.

CRITICAL THINKING Reflecting Look back at all the jobs you have learned about in this book. Which of these jobs are you interested in? Which job(s) do you think you are most suited for? Note your answers and reasons. Then share them with a partner.

_____

_____

VOCABULARY REVIEW

Do you remember the meanings of these words? Check (✓) the ones you know. Look back at the unit and review any words you're not sure of.

Reading A

☐ collector   ☐ illegal*   ☐ in demand   ☐ law   ☐ locate*
☐ preserve   ☐ treasure   ☐ valuable   ☐ weigh   ☐ worth

Reading B

☐ capable*   ☐ destroy   ☐ employ   ☐ equipment* ☐ height
☐ limited   ☐ majority*   ☐ middle   ☐ occupation* ☐ race

* Academic Word List

10

UNCOVERING THE PAST

Chichén Itzá, in Mexico, was a major city of the Maya people from A.D. 750 to 1200. It contains stepped pyramids and other stone structures.

WARM UP

Discuss these questions with a partner.

1. What are some famous ancient sites or monuments? Make a list.

2. Which of the places you've listed would you most like to visit? Why?

BEFORE YOU READ

DEFINITIONS **A.** Read the caption below. Use the correct form of the words in **bold** to complete these definitions (1–3).

1. _____ are scientists who study the buildings, tools, and other _____ of people who lived in the past.

2. A(n) _____ is a place where a dead person is buried.

3. A(n) _____ is a brave and experienced soldier or fighter.

PREDICTING **B.** Look at the photo on page 134. Why do you think the soldiers today are no longer in full color? Read the passage to check your ideas.

﹀ In 1974, farmers digging a well in Xi'an, China, uncovered clay soldiers that had been hidden for more than 2,000 years. Since then, **archeologists** have found about 8,000 more of these soldiers, along with other **artifacts**. The life-sized **warriors** were meant to guard the **tomb** of China's first ruler. This image shows what they originally looked like.

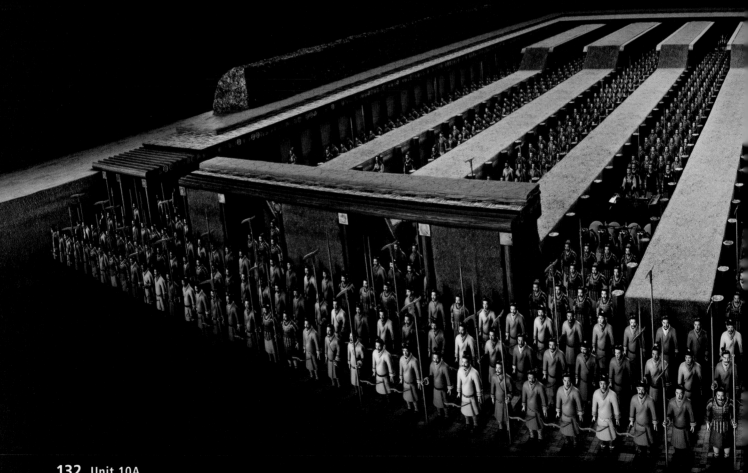

THE ARMY'S
TRUE COLORS

A The first emperor[1] of China, Qin Shihuang, is remembered for the many things he did during his rule. Between 221 and 210 B.C., he started the **construction** of the Great Wall of China. He built a large **network** of roads. He introduced a new writing system, **currency**, and set of measurements. The emperor also ordered the construction of a huge **army** of life-sized terracotta[2] soldiers. These, he hoped, would **protect** his tomb after his death.

---

1 An **emperor** is a leader who rules a group of regions or countries.
2 **Terracotta** is a type of clay used for making things such as flower pots, small statues, and tiles.

Lost in Time

B Today, the soldiers in Xi'an's terracotta museum are light brown, but they weren't always this color. They began as an army of red, blue, yellow, green, white, and purple. Sadly, most of the colors did not **last** to the present day. Before their discovery, the clay soldiers were protected by being underground. When they were unearthed, however, the air caused the coating under the paint to fall off. The paint disappeared in less time than it takes to boil an egg, taking with it important pieces of history.

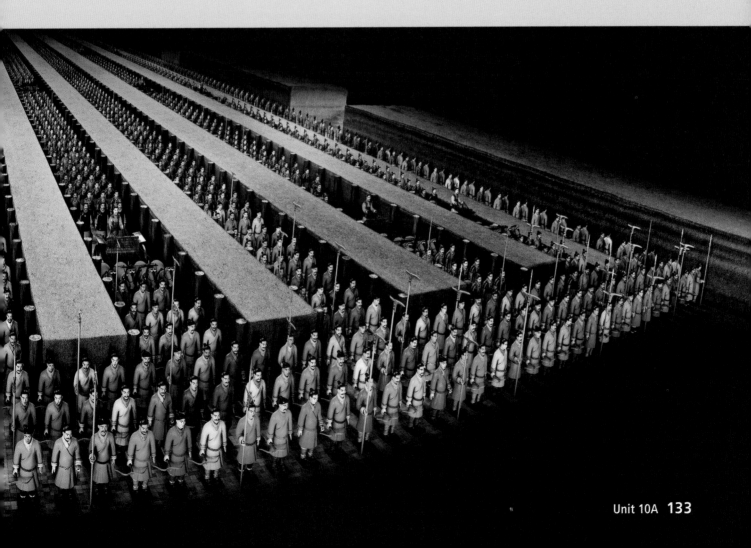

New Techniques

C   New **techniques** are now starting to **reveal** the army's true colors. Archeologists have recently discovered an area with more than a hundred soldiers. Many of these still have their painted features, including black hair, pink faces, and black or brown eyes. Chinese and German researchers have developed a special **liquid** to help preserve the soldiers' colors. After they find a soldier or other artifact, archeologists spray it with the liquid. They then cover it in plastic.

Back to Life

D   Archeologists are also finding colors in the dirt around Xi'an's terracotta warriors. It's important not to disturb the dirt, so the colors won't be lost. "We are treating the earth as an artifact," says archeologist Rong Bo, the museum's leading chemist. The next challenge, says Rong, is to find a way to **apply** the colors to the army again. Once that happens, artists can bring Emperor Qin's army back to life in full color.

∨ **Pit 1—burial ground of the emperor's main army—contains more than 6,000 statues.**

A. Choose the best answer for each question.

GIST **1.** What is the reading mainly about?

   a. how the emperor's tomb was built
   b. the original colors of the terracotta soldiers
   c. what life was like for soldiers under Emperor Qin

MAIN IDEA **2.** What is the main idea of paragraph B?

   a. The soldiers lost their colors very quickly after being discovered.
   b. The soldiers' paint fell off because of the high temperature.
   c. Visitors to the museum do not actually see the original soldiers.

VOCABULARY **3.** In paragraph B, what does the word *unearthed* mean?

   a. destroyed   b. dug up   c. identified

DETAIL **4.** What have archeologists recently discovered?

   a. a place with over a hundred terracotta warriors
   b. a liquid in the tomb that preserves the soldiers' colors
   c. a new tomb for Emperor Qin

INFERENCE **5.** Which statement would Rong Bo probably agree with?

   a. The soldiers should be left the way they were found.
   b. Artists should be able to paint the soldiers any color they want.
   c. We should try to restore the army's original colors.

⌃ **Emperor Qin ordered that every clay soldier be completely unique, so each soldier has different facial features.**

SUMMARIZING **B.** Complete the concept map with words from the reading.

Review this reading skill in Unit 4A

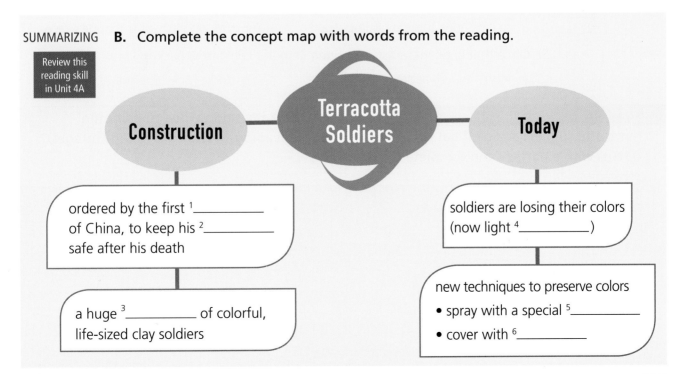

Construction

Terracotta Soldiers

Today

ordered by the first ¹_____ of China, to keep his ²_____ safe after his death

a huge ³_____ of colorful, life-sized clay soldiers

soldiers are losing their colors (now light ⁴_____)

new techniques to preserve colors
• spray with a special ⁵_____
• cover with ⁶_____

Finding Meaning (2)—Identifying Homonyms

When you read, you will often come across homonyms—words that have the same spelling and pronunciation, but have different meanings. Knowing the different possible meanings will improve your overall comprehension. You can usually tell the correct definition of a word by identifying its part of speech and by using the context (the words around it). For example:

back (*n.*) a body part: *My **back** hurts from moving furniture all day.* (*adv.*) the opposite way from the one you are facing or traveling: *She took a step **back** when the dog barked at her.*

part (*n.*) a piece of something that can be combined to make a whole: *The story had many **parts** to it.* (*v.*) to separate from someone: *They were very sad to **part** after a long journey together.*

DEFINITIONS **A.** Read these sentences from Reading A. For each word in **bold**, identify the part of speech and use the context to decide which definition (a or b) is correct.

1. The first emperor of China, Qin Shihuang, is remembered for the many things he did during his **rule**.

   a. (*n.*) a law   b. (*n.*) a period of control

2. He introduced a new writing system, currency, and **set** of measurements.

   a. (*n.*) a group of similar things   b. (*v.*) to put in place

3. Today, the soldiers in Xi'an's terracotta museum are **light** brown.

   a. (*adj.*) not dark   b. (*adj.*) not heavy

4. Many of these still have their painted **features**, including black hair, pink faces, and black or brown eyes.

   a. (*v.*) includes something important   b. (*pl. n.*) parts of someone's face

5. **Once** that happens, artists can bring Emperor Qin's army back to life in full color.

   a. (*conj.*) when; as soon as   b. (*adv.*) one time only

CRITICAL THINKING Evaluating Pros and Cons   Do you think it's a good idea to paint the terracotta soldiers again? What could be some pros (advantages) and cons (disadvantages)? Discuss with a partner and complete the chart below.

Pros	Cons

COMPLETION **A.** Circle the correct words to complete the information below.

The tomb of Emperor Qin Shihuang was ¹**constructed** / **revealed** more than 2,000 years ago and has never been opened. This is because archeologists, as well as the Chinese government, want to ²**apply** / **protect** what lies inside it.

⌃ **A terracotta horse**

Many archeologists feel we don't have the ³**currency** / **techniques** right now to preserve whatever is found there. Once unearthed, the artifacts may lose their original colors, much like the emperor's terracotta ⁴**network** / **army**.

Modern tests have also ⁵**applied** / **revealed** high levels of mercury—a ⁶**liquid** / **technique** metal—in the area. It is thought that Emperor Qin's tomb is surrounded by a ⁷**currency** / **network** of rivers filled with mercury, which symbolized never-ending life.

WORDS IN CONTEXT **B.** Complete each sentence with the correct answer (a or b).

1. If an event, situation, or problem **lasts** for a particular length of time, it _____ for that length of time.

   a. continues to exist   b. stops happening

2. A country's **currency** refers to its _____.

   a. people   b. money

3. If you **apply** paint to something, you _____.

   a. put it on   b. remove it

COLLOCATIONS **C.** The phrases in the box are often used with the word **reveal**. Complete the sentences with the correct phrases from the box.

a secret	**the cause**	**the truth**

1. You should never reveal _____ a friend shares with you.

2. Archeology can reveal _____ about how ancient societies lived and worked.

3. An autopsy is a medical examination of a dead body. The purpose of an autopsy is to reveal _____ of death.

BEFORE YOU READ

QUIZ **A.** What do you know about the Giza pyramids in Egypt? Read the sentences below and circle **T** (true) or **F** (false). Then check your answers on page 144.

1. The pyramids of Giza are older than the Mayan pyramids in   **T**   **F**
Chichén Itzá (see page 131).

2. When they were first built, the pyramids of Giza were white.   **T**   **F**

3. The Great Pyramid of Khufu at Giza was the world's tallest structure for   **T**   **F**
over 3,000 years.

SKIMMING **B.** Read the caption below and skim the passage. Who do you think built the Giza pyramids? Circle a, b, c, or d. Then read the passage to check your answer.

a. foreign workers   c. Egyptian workers
b. foreign slaves   d. Egyptian slaves

Close to the Giza pyramids **(A)**, an ancient city has been unearthed **(B)**. Archeologists believe the people who built the pyramids once lived there; their tombs are hidden a short distance away **(C)**.

WONDERS
OF EGYPT

A Many people today think of the pyramids of Giza as the defining **icon** of ancient Egyptian culture. But who actually built them? For years, we did not know for sure. Now, however, archeologists have discovered an ancient city near the pyramids. Close by, there is a cemetery where the pyramid builders were buried. From studying these places, archeologists can now **confirm** that the pyramids were not built by slaves[1] or foreigners (or space aliens!). **Ordinary** Egyptians built them.

B It took about 80 years to build the pyramids. Archeologists believe that about 20,000–30,000 people were **involved** in the construction. The workers had different **roles**. Some dug up the rock, some moved it, and some shaped it into **blocks**. People also worked on different teams, each with its own name. Workers often **competed** to see whose team could do a job faster.

C Life for these workers was hard. "We can see that in their skeletons," says Azza Mohamed Sarry El-Din, a scientist studying bones found in the cemetery. **According to** her research, the bones show signs of arthritis.[2] This probably developed from carrying heavy things for a long time. Archeologists have also found many female skeletons in the ancient city and cemetery. The damage to their bones is similar to that of the men. In fact, their lives may have been even tougher: Male workers generally lived to age 40–45, but women to only 30–35. However, workers usually had enough food, and they also received medical care if they got sick or hurt.

D The **task** was challenging, but laborers were **proud** of their work. On a wall in Khufu's Great Pyramid, for example, a group of workers wrote *Friends of Khufu*. "It's because they were not just building the tomb of their king," says Egyptian archeologist Zahi Hawass. "They were building Egypt. It was a national project, and everyone was a participant."[3]

---

1 A **slave** is a person who is legally owned by someone else and has to work for that person.

2 **Arthritis** is a medical condition that causes the hips, knees, and other joints in the body to hurt.

3 A **participant** is a person who joins a certain activity.

A. Choose the best answer for each question.

PURPOSE

1. The main purpose of this reading is to describe _____.

a. who the pyramid builders were and what they did
b. what makes the pyramids of Giza special
c. why Egyptian kings wanted to build pyramids

GIST

2. What is paragraph C mainly about?

a. information on the lives of pyramid builders
b. the benefits of being a male worker
c. the roles of men and women in ancient Egyptian society

REFERENCE

3. Who does *their* refer to in paragraph C, line 6 (*In fact, their lives may* …)?

a. archeologists
b. male workers
c. female workers

VOCABULARY

4. In paragraph D, what does the word *laborers* mean?

a. kings
b. workers
c. women

⌃ **The Great Pyramid of Khufu—the oldest and largest of the Giza pyramids—is made up of more than two million blocks of stone.**

INFERENCE

5. What can we infer about the people who wrote *Friends of Khufu* on a wall?

a. They were looking for new friends.
b. They were pleased with their work.
c. They got into trouble for writing on the wall.

EVALUATING STATEMENTS

B. Are the following statements true or false according to the reading passage, or is the information not given? Circle **T** (true), **F** (false), or **NG** (not given).

1. It took more than a hundred years to complete construction of the pyramids.   T   F   NG

2. The rocks were shaped into blocks mostly by women.   T   F   NG

3. The pyramid builders worked in teams.   T   F   NG

4. Male workers generally lived longer than female workers.   T   F   NG

Creating an Outline Summary

Previously, we looked at how to annotate a text by making notes in the margins (see Unit 9B Reading Skill). Another way to organize your thoughts as you read is to create an outline summary. This is helpful when dealing with large amounts of information. To create an outline, first pick out the main ideas of the text. Next, write down the subtopic(s)—what the author says about each main idea. Lastly, write the details given about each subtopic (usually two or three).

OUTLINING **A.** Use these notes about Reading B to complete the outline below.

| national project | ordinary Egyptians | 80 years | arthritis |
| teams and roles | 30–35 years | medical care | proud |

OUTLINE: Wonders of Egypt

1. Construction of the pyramids
   a. Built by [1]_____
   b. Time extent and jobs
      - took about [2]_____ to build
      - 20,000–30,000 people involved
      - people worked in different [3]_____
2. Builders' lives and attitudes
   a. Hard life
      - bones show signs of [4]_____
      - men lived to 40–45 years, women [5]_____
   b. Food and health
      - had enough food
      - had access to [6]_____
   c. Attitude of laborers
      - felt [7]_____ of their work
      - saw it as a(n) [8]_____

CRITICAL THINKING Analyzing Evidence   Does the author think the pyramid builders had mostly positive or negative feelings about their work? What evidence does the author give? Discuss with a partner and note your ideas.

_____

_____

COMPLETION **A.** Circle the correct words to complete the information below.

Cleopatra (69–30 B.C.) became queen of Egypt at age 18, when her brother became king. The pair [1]**competed / confirmed** for control of Egypt, and Cleopatra lost. Later, two important leaders from Rome—Julius Caesar and Marc Antony—both fell in love with her. [2]**Involved / According to** legend, Cleopatra was beautiful and very smart. With the help of Caesar and Antony, she regained control of Egypt and played an important [3]**role / block** in society.

Staying in power, however, was not an easy [4]**role / task**. Cleopatra had many enemies[1] who eventually took power from her. In the end, the queen was too [5]**ordinary / proud** to surrender[2] and instead chose to kill herself. But her legend survived, and today Cleopatra remains a(n) [6]**icon / task** of ancient Egypt.

∧ **Experts believe that this marble bust may represent Cleopatra.**

1 An **enemy** is someone who wants to harm you.
2 If you **surrender**, you stop fighting and admit you have lost.

DEFINITIONS **B.** Use the words in **red** in activity A to complete these definitions (1–5).

1. If something is _____, it is common or usual.

2. A(n) _____ is an activity or piece of work that you have to do.

3. If something is _____, it is shown to be true.

4. A(n) _____ is a large solid piece of hard material (e.g., rock, stone) with flat sides. It is usually square or rectangular in shape.

5. If you are _____ in a situation or activity, you are taking part in it or are connected with it.

COLLOCATIONS **C.** The words in the box are often used with the word **task**. Complete the sentences with the correct words from the box. One word is extra.

complete	give	impossible	simple

1. No one can do this—it's a(n) _____ task.

2. A few students were unable to _____ the task before the deadline.

3. The boss decided to _____ the team a new task to do.

CITY IN THE CLOUDS

∨ Machu Picchu,
Peru

BEFORE YOU WATCH

PREVIEWING **A.** Read the information. The words in **bold** appear in the video. Match these words with their definitions (1–4).

South America is home to many important archeological sites. But few are as grand as the ancient Inca city of Machu Picchu, located high in the Andes Mountains in Peru. The city's centuries-old palaces, plazas, temples, and water channels are connected by a network of narrow lanes or paths. Each **aspect** of Machu Picchu was well planned, with impressive **engineering** techniques. There have been many theories about why the Inca people built this site, but its original purpose is still unknown. Nevertheless, archeologists continue to study the **ruins**. Modern research may one day reveal the true purpose and uses of Machu Picchu, and help us learn more about the great Inca **empire**.

1. _____ : a group of nations ruled by one person or government

2. _____ : one part of a situation, idea, or plan

3. _____ : the parts of a building or city that remain after the rest has fallen down or been destroyed

4. _____ : the work involved in designing and constructing machines and other structures (e.g., roads, bridges)

COMPLETION **A. Read the notes below. Then watch the video and complete these notes.**

1. Construction of Machu Picchu
    a. Built by the Inca people over ¹_____ years ago
    b. Impressive engineering
        • buildings were made out of ²_____, without the help of wheels or ³_____ tools
        • walls were built such that they remain undamaged by ⁴_____
2. Discovery and later developments
    a. 1911: Became known to the outside world when a local ⁵_____ showed the site to Hiram Bingham
    b. ⁶_____: Named as one of the "new Seven Wonders of the World"

CRITICAL THINKING Justifying an Opinion   **Discuss these questions with a partner.**

▶ Hiram Bingham removed about 5,000 artifacts from Machu Picchu and kept them in a museum at Yale University. Do you think this was a good idea, or should the artifacts have been left where they were found? Give reasons for your opinion.

▶ How does your opinion compare with your answer to the Critical Thinking question on page 122?

VOCABULARY REVIEW

Do you remember the meanings of these words? Check (✓) the ones you know. Look back at the unit and review any words you're not sure of.

Reading A

☐ apply   ☐ army   ☐ construction*   ☐ currency*   ☐ last

☐ liquid   ☐ network*   ☐ protect   ☐ reveal*   ☐ technique*

Reading B

☐ according to   ☐ block   ☐ compete   ☐ confirm*   ☐ icon

☐ involved*   ☐ ordinary   ☐ proud   ☐ role*   ☐ task*

* Academic Word List

Answers to **Before You Read**, activity A, page 138:

1. True. The Giza pyramids were built over 4,000 years ago—starting in about 2550 B.C.
2. True. The top of one of the pyramids still has its white-colored covering.
3. True. It was the tallest structure for 3,800 years—until England's Lincoln Cathedral was completed in about A.D. 1300.

11

PLASTIC PLANET

WARM UP

Discuss these questions with a partner.

1. What do you think are some of the most important environmental issues today?

2. What are some things that your community is doing to help the environment?

Plastic bags are one of the biggest sources of trash in the ocean.

BEFORE YOU READ

UNDERSTANDING CHARTS AND GRAPHS

A. Look at the infographics. Then answer the questions below with a partner.

Review this reading skill in Unit 5A

1. What are some uses of plastic? What proportion of global plastic production is used for packaging?

2. Approximately how many tons of plastic were produced in 2015?

3. On average, how long are plastics in building and construction used before they are thrown away? How about for packaging?

PREDICTING

B. What kinds of problems do you think plastic waste (garbage) causes for the world's oceans? Note your ideas. Then check as you read the passage on page 148.

_____

_____

Almost 40 percent of plastic produced is for packaging (to cover goods). Some of this is recycled, but most is used just once and thrown away.

Global plastic production by industry: 2015 (in millions of tons)

72 Building and construction

52 Other

161 Packaging

65 Textiles

46 Consumer products

30 Transportation

19 Electrical

3 Industrial machinery

NGM STAFF. SOURCE: ROLAND GEYER, UNIVERSITY OF CALIFORNIA, SANTA BARBARA

We use plastic to make many things, from medical equipment to TVs to food packaging. At the end of their useful life, most plastic products are thrown away. These plastics then break down into smaller pieces that can last for centuries. This causes problems, especially for the world's oceans.

The growth of global plastic production: 1950–2015
(in millions of tons)

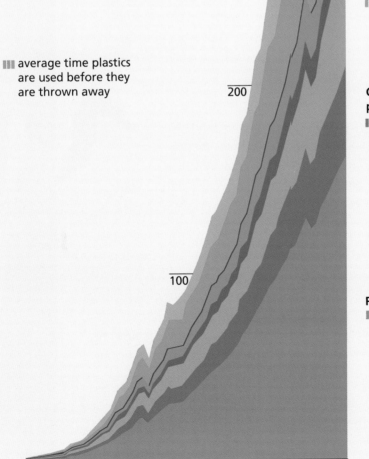

▮▮▮ average time plastics are used before they are thrown away

Total
448 million tons produced in 2015

Other
▮▮▮▮▮ 5 years

Building and construction
▮▮▮▮▮▮▮▮▮▮▮▮▮▮▮▮▮▮▮▮▮▮▮▮▮▮▮▮▮▮▮▮▮▮▮ 35 years

Industrial machinery
▮▮▮▮▮▮▮▮▮▮▮▮▮▮▮▮▮▮▮▮ 20 years

Transportation
▮▮▮▮▮▮▮▮▮▮▮▮▮ 13 years

Electrical
▮▮▮▮▮▮▮▮ 8 years

Textiles
▮▮▮▮▮ 5 years

Consumer products
▮▮▮ 3 years

Packaging
▮ Less than 6 months

JASON TREAT AND RYAN T. WILLIAMS, NGM STAFF. SOURCE: ROLAND GEYER, UNIVERSITY OF CALIFORNIA, SANTA BARBARA

THE PROBLEM
WITH PLASTIC

A On a boat near Costa Rica, a team of marine biologists[1] is helping a turtle. The animal is having trouble breathing, and the team discovers why—there is something inside its nose. A scientist tries to **extract** the object, but the turtle cries in pain. Finally, after eight long minutes, a long object is pulled out: It is a 10-centimeter plastic straw.

B The video of the turtle's **rescue** has been viewed millions of times on YouTube. It has helped raise awareness of a growing problem: The world's seas are full of plastic. Since 2000, there has been a **huge** increase in worldwide plastic production, but we **recycle** less than one-fifth of it. A lot of this plastic waste ends up in the ocean. Today, scientists think about 8.1 billion kilograms goes into the sea every year from coastal regions. Most of this plastic will never biodegrade.[2]

C This ocean plastic hurts millions of sea animals every year. Some fish eat plastic because it is covered with sea plants, and it looks and smells like food. **Typically**, eating plastic leads to **constant** hunger. "Imagine you ate lunch and then just felt **weak** … and hungry all day," says marine biologist Matthew Savoca. "That would be very **confusing**." In some cases, eating sharp pieces of plastic can seriously hurt sea animals and even result in death.

D Plastic is useful to people because it is strong and lasts a long time—but this is bad news for sea creatures who eat or get stuck in it. According to Savoca, "Single-use plastics are the worst." These are items that are used only once before we throw them away. Some **common** examples include straws, water bottles, and plastic bags. About 700 sea species (including the turtle from the video) have been caught in or have eaten this kind of plastic. Luckily, the turtle survived and was released back into the ocean.

E How will plastic affect sea animals in the **long term**? "I think we'll know the answers in 5 to 10 years' time," says Debra Lee Magadini from Columbia University. But by then, another 25 million tons of plastic will already be in the ocean.

⌄ **A seahorse clutches a plastic cotton swab.**

---

1 A **marine biologist** is a scientist who studies sea life.
2 If something **biodegrades**, it breaks into little pieces and goes away completely.

READING COMPREHENSION

A. Choose the best answer for each question.

GIST

1. What could be another title for this reading?

    a. The Work of Marine Biologists

    b. Dangers Facing Sea Turtles

    c. How Plastic Harms Sea Creatures

DETAIL

2. Which of these questions is NOT answered in paragraph A?

    a. What was the cause of the turtle's pain?

    b. What tools did the scientists use to remove the object?

    c. Where did the incident take place?

REFERENCE

3. What does *It* refer to in the second sentence of paragraph B?

    a. the video

    b. the turtle

    c. YouTube

INFERENCE

4. Which of the following objects is a single-use item?

    a. a plastic toothbrush

    b. a plastic fork

    c. a plastic comb

INFERENCE

5. Which of these can we definitely say about ocean plastic?

    a. 8.1 billion kilograms of plastic waste goes into the sea every year from coastal regions.

    b. The plastic waste in the ocean hurts sea animals and can even kill them.

    c. Scientists will have a clear understanding of the ocean's plastic problem in 5 to 10 years' time.

∧ Single-use plastics have become a major global concern. In 2018, Collins Dictionary named "single-use" as its Word of the Year.

EVALUATING STATEMENTS

B. Are the following statements true or false according to the reading passage, or is the information not given? Circle T (true), F (false), or NG (not given).

1. Many people have watched the video of the turtle on YouTube.	**T**	**F**	**NG**
2. Most of the plastic in the ocean is biodegradable.	**T**	**F**	**NG**
3. Matthew Savoca was a member of the team that found the turtle.	**T**	**F**	**NG**
4. The turtle in the video died from its injuries.	**T**	**F**	**NG**
5. Half the world's plastics are made in Asia.	**T**	**F**	**NG**

Understanding a Writer's Use of Quotes

A writer may choose to include the exact words from a source. These are set off by quotation marks
(" "). Quotes can be used for various reasons, such as the following:

- To add a supporting statement or question:
  *Locals aren't waiting for the government to solve the plastic problem. "It's important for us to start
  cleaning up the oceans ourselves," said one resident.*

- To provide expert evidence for an argument:
  *The plastic in our oceans will not go away by itself. "We see plastic dating back to the 1960s and
  1970s," says Boyan Slat, CEO of the nonprofit group Ocean Cleanup.*

- To highlight an interesting or memorable phrase:
  *"Ghost nets" are fishing nets (usually made of plastic) that have been left or lost in the ocean. Every
  year, they trap and kill millions of sea animals.*

SCANNING **A.** Look back at Reading A. Underline the quotes. Discuss with a partner: Why did
the writer include them?

IDENTIFYING
PURPOSE
B. Match each of these quotes (1–4) with its purpose. Write a, b, or c. One option
is used twice.

a. to add a supporting statement or question
b. to provide expert evidence for an argument
c. to highlight an interesting or memorable phrase

_____ **1.** The problem of plastics in our oceans is bigger than most people realize.
"What's floating on the surface … is only 3 percent of the plastics that enters
the ocean every single year," says Eben Schwartz from the California Coastal
Commission.

_____ **2.** It's important that everyone uses less plastic. "My class recently decided to
stop using plastic straws," says 12-year-old Molly Peterson.

_____ **3.** The Great Pacific Garbage Patch is a collection of floating trash that covers a huge
area of the North Pacific Ocean. However, it's more "plastic soup" than patch.

_____ **4.** Ocean plastic is a big problem for people who rely on fish and seafood for
their diets. "How can we be sure that the fish we catch or buy is safe to eat?"
asks local resident Mayumi Fujikawa.

CRITICAL THINKING Inferring Effects   Reading A looks at how plastic in the ocean affects sea
animals. In what ways does this ocean plastic affect humans? Discuss with a partner and note
your ideas.

_____

_____

COMPLETION

A. Complete the paragraph with words from the box.

common	huge	recycle	rescue

The Owl ¹_____ Centre is a nonprofit organization in South Africa that is dedicated to the protection of owls. It has also been doing incredible work for the environment. In 2018, the center started a project to collect used plastic bottles and ²_____ them into owl houses. Plastic bottles are an increasingly ³_____ sight in our rivers and oceans. By reusing these plastic bottles, the center can build more nesting boxes for owls and also ensure that less plastic ends up in the ocean. The project has been a ⁴_____ success, and the center is now raising money to buy a ship that will collect plastic directly from the ocean.

∧ **An owl house made from recycled plastic**

WORDS IN CONTEXT

B. Complete the sentences. Circle the correct words.

1. If you **extract** something, you *buy it / take it out*.

2. You use **typically** to refer to what *usually happens / once happened* in a situation.

3. If someone is **weak**, they are not very *strong / intelligent*.

4. Something that is **confusing** is *easy / difficult* for people to understand.

5. You use **constant** to describe something that happens *some of / all* the time.

6. Something that happens over the **long term** will *happen very soon / continue far into the future*.

WORD PARTS

C. The prefix *ex-* means "out" or "out of" (e.g., extract). Complete the sentences using the words in the box. One word is extra.

except	exit	extend	extract

1. "Ghost nets" are a serious problem along Australia's northern coastline; they can _____ for more than several hundred meters in length.

2. The store is open every day _____ Sunday.

3. Boyan Slat's foundation, Ocean Cleanup, is developing various technologies that can _____ plastic waste from our oceans.

BEFORE YOU READ

DISCUSSION   **A.** Read the caption below and look at the photo. What plastic items do you see in this photo? Are any of them single-use items? Discuss with a partner.

PREDICTING   **B.** How can you use less plastic in your day-to-day life? Note some ideas. Then read the passage and check if any of your ideas are mentioned.

_____

_____

⌄ **Plastic garbage collected from a beach in North East England, U.K.**

FIVE TIPS FOR USING LESS PLASTIC

A The world has a plastic problem—and it is increasing. Scientists are working to find a long-term solution by making plastic more biodegradable. But in the meantime, here are five things you can do to **reduce** plastic waste now.

A reusable shopping bag

B **1. *Quit using plastic bags.*** Instead, take your own reusable shopping bag to the store. People use a trillion[1] plastic bags worldwide every year. Roughly 10 percent are used in the United States alone. That's almost one bag per American per day. In contrast, the average Dane uses four single-use bags *per year*. In 1993, Denmark was the first country to place a **tax** on plastic bags. Today, other countries (such as Chile, Kenya, Indonesia, Germany, and New Zealand) either make **customers** pay for plastic bags, or have **banned** them completely.

C **2. *Skip the straw.*** Today, around 8.3 billion plastic straws **pollute** the world's beaches. So when you order a drink, say *no* to the straw, or bring your own reusable one. In 2018, Seattle became the first major U.S. city to ban plastic straws, and many other cities are set to follow its example.

A metal, reusable straw

D **3. *Don't use plastic bottles.*** Buy a reusable bottle and fill it with any type of beverage you like. Some cities, like Bundanoon in Australia and San Francisco in the U.S., have completely or partially banned bottled water. **Globally**, however, people still buy nearly a million plastic bottles every minute.

A reusable bottle

E **4. *Avoid plastic packaging.*** Buy bar soap instead of liquid soap in plastic **containers**. Don't buy fruit or vegetables in plastic packaging. In the United Kingdom, leaders are calling for[2] supermarkets to have plastic-free areas. They also want to tax plastic take-out containers.

F **5. *Recycle.*** We can't recycle all plastic items, but it is possible to recycle most bottles and milk or juice cartons. Today, Norway recycles 97 percent of its plastic bottles. How? Machines at most supermarkets take the bottles and give a **refund** of up to 2.5 kroner (32 cents) per bottle.

---

1 1 **trillion** = 1,000,000,000,000 or 1,000 billion
2 If you **call for** something to happen, you make a strong request for it to happen.

A. Choose the best answer for each question.

GIST

1. This passage generally consists of _____ .

a. suggestions   b. reasons   c. predictions

DETAIL

2. How many plastic bags are used in the United States every year?

a. about 10 billion   b. about 100 billion   c. a trillion

VOCABULARY

3. In paragraph B, what does *average* mean?

a. typical or usual   b. smart or intelligent   c. responsible or careful

DETAIL

4. According to the passage, which of the following should we NOT do?

a. buy a reusable bag   b. get a metal straw   c. use liquid soap

REFERENCE

5. What does *They* refer to in the last sentence of paragraph E?

a. plastic-free areas   b. supermarkets   c. U.K. leaders

SUMMARIZING

Review this reading skill in Unit 4A

B. Complete the concept map with the correct city or country names from the passage.

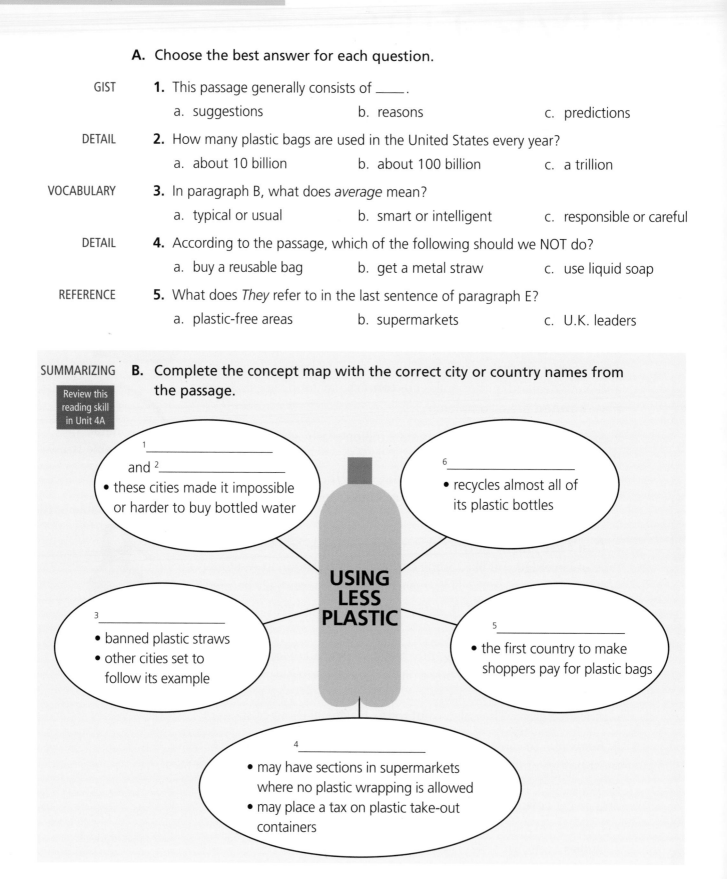

1 _____ and 2 _____
- these cities made it impossible or harder to buy bottled water

6 _____
- recycles almost all of its plastic bottles

3 _____
- banned plastic straws
- other cities set to follow its example

USING LESS PLASTIC

5 _____
- the first country to make shoppers pay for plastic bags

4 _____
- may have sections in supermarkets where no plastic wrapping is allowed
- may place a tax on plastic take-out containers

Finding Meaning (3)—Using Context

When you come across an unfamiliar word, first see if it is defined within the text or in a glossary (see Unit 7B Reading Skill). If it is not, you can check its meaning in a dictionary, or look at the context—the words and sentences around it—to guess its meaning. To guess the meaning of a word from context, first identify the word's part of speech (noun, verb, etc.). Then look to see if there are synonyms, antonyms, or examples in the sentence or the sentences before and after it that can help you determine its meaning.

SCANNING **A.** Look back at Reading B. Find and underline the words in **bold** below (1–5).

WORDS IN CONTEXT **B.** Now look at the context around each of the words in the passage. Choose the option that is closest in meaning to each word.

1. **roughly** (paragraph B)

   a. only　　　　　　　b. unfortunately　　　　　c. approximately

2. **skip** (paragraph C)

   a. share　　　　　　　b. reuse　　　　　　　　c. stop using

3. **beverage** (paragraph D)

   a. food　　　　　　　b. drink　　　　　　　　c. bottle

4. **partially** (paragraph D)

   a. in part　　　　　　b. totally　　　　　　　c. easily

5. **cartons** (paragraph F)

   a. straws　　　　　　b. containers　　　　　　c. bags

CRITICAL THINKING Ranking Suggestions　Rank the five tips 1–5 (1 = easiest to do; 5 = hardest to do). Then compare answers with a partner and give reasons for your answers.

_____ Quit using plastic bags.

_____ Skip the straw.

_____ Recycle.

_____ Avoid plastic packaging.

_____ Don't use plastic bottles.

A worker sorts plastic bottles at a recycling center in Wuhan, China.

COMPLETION **A.** Complete the information with words from the box.

containers	customers	globally	reduce	tax

The small nation of Wales has been working to ¹_____ plastic waste for years. In 2011, the government introduced a law requiring all supermarkets and large stores to charge a small fee for every single-use plastic bag used. By 2015, plastic bag use had fallen by 71 percent. This fee is not a ²_____. The money raised goes to environmental projects, not to the government. Plastic bottles are also collected, and then reused or melted into new items. Furthermore, there are some shops in Wales that sell only plastic-free products. ³_____ can bring their own ⁴_____ and fill them with the items they buy.

In 2017, Wales ranked second ⁵_____ (just behind Germany) for recycling household waste, including household plastic. The country is now looking at ways to further improve its recycling systems, and may even become the world leader for recycling in the near future.

DEFINITIONS **B.** Complete the definitions below with words from the box.

avoid	bans	pollute	quit	refund

1. If you _____ an activity, you stop doing it.

2. If a government _____ something (e.g., a movie or product), it must not be shown or used.

3. When you _____ water, air, or land, you make it dirty and dangerous to live in or to use.

4. If you _____ a person or thing, you stay away from them.

5. A(n) _____ is a sum of money that is returned to you.

COLLOCATIONS **C.** The words in the box are often used with the word **global**. Complete the sentences with the correct words from the box. One word is extra.

awareness	brand	problem	warming

1. Research shows that many plastics give off greenhouse gases as they break down, contributing to global _____.

2. Air pollution is a serious global _____.

3. The campaign helped raise global _____ of environmental issues.

OUR PLASTIC
WORLD

> Streetside trash at
Brick Lane Market,
London

BEFORE YOU WATCH

PREVIEWING **A.** Read the information. The words in **bold** appear in the video. Match these words with their definitions below.

Few of us can go a day without using something made of plastic. Most modern plastics are **synthetic**, and are made from fossil fuels. These synthetic plastics are useful because they are easy to shape and can last a long time. However, they take several hundred years to biodegrade, which can be bad for the environment. If people throw plastic items on the ground or into rivers, they can end up in the sea. This has a terrible **impact** on sea animals and can eventually **ruin** our oceans. Scientists are now working to find nonsynthetic **alternatives**—called bioplastics—that can help reduce plastic pollution.

1. synthetic •   • a. option; other possibility

2. impact •   • b. not natural; man-made

3. ruin •   • c. a strong or powerful effect

4. alternative •   • d. to harm or destroy something

DISCUSSION **B.** Work with a partner. Make a list of the objects around you that are made of plastic. How many plastic things do you use in a day? What do you do with them after using them?

COMPLETION   **A. Look at the chart below. Then watch the video and complete the chart.**

Synthetic plastics	Bioplastics
• made from fossil fuels (e.g., [1]_____)	• made from [3]_____ (e.g., a rubber tree)
• most of it ends up as trash, especially [2]_____ plastics	• can break down much [4]_____ than synthetic plastics

MULTIPLE CHOICE   **B. Watch the video again. Complete each sentence with the correct answer.**

1. The amount of plastics produced since 1950 is roughly the same _____ as 1,600 pyramids of Giza.

    a. weight   b. size

2. About _____ of all plastic waste comes from single-use plastics.

    a. 20 percent   b. 40 percent

3. According to the video, we can reduce plastic pollution by _____.

    a. placing a tax on synthetic plastics and making bioplastics cheaper
    b. avoiding single-use plastic products and creating more bioplastics

CRITICAL THINKING Applying Ideas   Imagine you want to start a campaign in your area to reduce plastic waste. Think about the tips and solutions in this unit. Which would you focus on? Note your ideas below and describe the project to a partner.

Your project name: _____

Project's purpose/focus: _____

Actions required: _____

_____

VOCABULARY REVIEW

Do you remember the meanings of these words? Check (✓) the ones you know. Look back at the unit and review any words you're not sure of.

Reading A

☐ common   ☐ confusing   ☐ constant*   ☐ extract*   ☐ huge

☐ long term   ☐ recycle   ☐ rescue   ☐ typically   ☐ weak

Reading B

☐ avoid   ☐ ban   ☐ container   ☐ customer   ☐ globally*

☐ pollute   ☐ quit   ☐ reduce   ☐ refund   ☐ tax

* Academic Word List

VANISHED!

12

Pilot Amelia Earhart in 1931, six years before she went missing

WARM UP

Discuss these questions with a partner.

1. Do you know of any famous explorers? What places did they visit?

2. Can you think of any famous people who vanished (went missing) or died mysteriously?

BEFORE YOU READ

COMPLETION   **A.** What do you know about the world's highest mountain—known locally as Qomolangma, and more widely as Mount Everest? Complete the information below with answers from the box. Two answers are extra.

| 8,850 | 1953 | oxygen | India | 200 | Nepal | cold | 4 |

- *Height:* [1]_____m; each year, it rises by another [2]_____mm.
- *First people to reach the summit (top):* Tenzing Norgay (a Sherpa from [3]_____) and Edmund Hillary (from New Zealand), in May [4]_____.
- *Health risks:* Because of the extreme [5]_____, climbers can get frostbite, especially on their fingers and toes.
- *Equipment:* Most climbers carry [6]_____ tanks to help them breathe.

PREDICTING   **B.** Look at the title on the next page and read paragraph A. What do you think the passage will be about? Read to check your predictions.

MYSTERY ON THE MOUNTAIN

A Were Edmund Hillary and Tenzing Norgay really the first people to reach the top of the world's highest mountain? Some believe that British climbers George Mallory and Andrew Irvine reached the summit before them in June 1924. **Unfortunately**, this is difficult to **prove** because both men vanished somewhere high on the mountain.

The world's highest mountain: Mount Everest (Qomolangma)

A Body in the Snow

B In 1999, a team of climbers visited the mountain, hoping to solve this mystery. Near the First Step, on the way to the summit, the team found Mallory's oxygen tank—**evidence** that he and Irvine had been near the top. Close by, a member of the team—Conrad Anker—discovered Mallory's body.

C When the team examined Mallory's body, they found items like a knife and matches, but no photos. Why is this important? Mallory had carried a photo of his wife with him. He had planned to leave the photo at the top of the mountain, if he reached it.

First to the Top?

D Did Mallory and Irvine **achieve** their goal and reach the summit? Probably not, according to Anker. Here are some reasons for his conclusion.

E **Difficult path / Poor equipment:** Mallory and Irvine were last seen near the mountain's Second Step. This is a 27-meter wall of rock. Climbing this **section** is extremely difficult, even with modern climbing equipment. Without the right tools, it is **unlikely** that Mallory and Irvine were able to continue to the top.

F **No frostbite:** Mallory and Irvine were seen near the summit late in the day. Climbers who reach the summit at this time need to **camp** at the top. If you do this, it is common to **suffer** from frostbite. But Mallory's body had no signs of frostbite.

G So what happened to Mallory and Irvine? Anker thinks they probably turned back just after the First Step. When Mallory was going down the mountain, perhaps he accidentally fell. Irvine's body has never been found. **Whatever** happened, they will always be remembered as early mountaineering heroes.[1]

___
1 A **hero** is someone who has done something brave, and who is therefore greatly admired.

George Mallory, photographed in 1909

The frozen remains of Mallory's body were discovered in 1999.

A. Choose the best answer for each question.

GIST

1. The reading is mainly about two climbers who _____ .

   a. solved a mystery about Edmund Hillary

   b. vanished while climbing a mountain

   c. recreated Hillary and Norgay's climb

INFERENCE

2. A reasonable conclusion from paragraphs B and C is that _____ .

   a. Mallory may have reached the top

   b. Mallory probably didn't reach the top

   c. the body discovered was not Mallory's

DETAIL

3. Which of these statements is true?

   a. Mallory's body showed signs of frostbite.

   b. Conrad Anker's team found two bodies on the mountain.

   c. Anker's team found some of Mallory's things on the mountain.

⌃ **Mallory and Irvine took a camera like this on their climb. However, the camera has never been found.**

VOCABULARY

4. If Mallory and Irvine *turned back* (paragraph G), they _____ the mountain.

   a. stopped and went down

   b. went around

   c. tried to walk up

INFERENCE

5. Which statement would Conrad Anker probably agree with?

   a. Both Mallory and Irvine reached the mountain's summit.

   b. Mallory and Irvine got close, but didn't reach the top.

   c. Irvine probably reached the top, but not Mallory.

CLASSIFYING

B. Complete the Venn diagram. Match each answer (a–e) with the man or men it describes.

   a. went to the world's highest mountain in 1924

   b. climbed with a photo of his wife

   c. body was discovered in 1999

   d. body was never discovered

   e. last seen near the Second Step

George Mallory   **Both**   **Andrew Irvine**

Summarizing: Using a T-chart (2)

Writers sometimes present two sides of an argument—giving reasons for and against an idea. Sometimes they list all the reasons *for* first, followed by all the reasons *against*. To introduce the reasons, writers may use phrases such as *one reason is …* and *in addition …* .

To summarize this type of text, it can be useful to list the reasons for and against in two columns, like in a T-chart (see Unit 5B Reading Skill). This helps readers evaluate the writer's arguments.

ANALYZING **A.** Look back at Reading A. Find and underline evidence that suggests George Mallory and Andrew Irvine reached the summit. Then circle the reasons against this being true.

SUMMARIZING **B.** Complete the chart below with words from Reading A.

Did Mallory and Irvine reach the mountain's summit?

Reasons for	Reasons against
• Anker's team discovered Mallory's [1]_____ tank and [2]_____ near First Step	• Second Step is very [5]_____ to climb, and Mallory and Irvine did not have modern climbing [6]_____
• team didn't find a(n) [3]_____ of Mallory's wife—he had planned to [4]_____ it at the summit	• no signs of [7]_____ on Mallory's body—it is [8]_____ for people to suffer from this if they camp near the summit for the night

CRITICAL THINKING Evaluating Evidence

▶ Based on the evidence in the reading, do you think Mallory and Irvine reached the top of the world's highest mountain? Why or why not? Compare your answers with a partner.

▶ What other evidence or information could help solve this mystery? Discuss with a partner and note some ideas.

_____

_____

_____

VOCABULARY PRACTICE

COMPLETION **A.** Complete the paragraph with words from the box.

> achievement   path   proved   suffered   unfortunately

Erik Weihenmayer is an American adventurer. He was born with a medical condition that [1]_____ left him blind at age 13. But this has not stopped him from leading a full and exciting life. On May 25, 2001, Weihenmayer reached the top of Everest (Qomolangma). With this [2]_____, Weihenmayer [3]_____ that it is possible for people who cannot see to climb the world's highest mountain. Three years later, he led a group of blind Tibetan teenagers up the 7,045-meter Lhakpa Ri mountain. The [4]_____ to the top was very difficult. Because of lack of oxygen, some teens [5]_____ from extreme headaches. Although the group did not reach the summit, their amazing journey was made into a movie called *Blindsight*.

∧ **Blind mountaineer Erik Weihenmayer**

WORDS IN CONTEXT **B.** Complete the sentences. Circle the correct words.

1. An example of **evidence** at a crime scene is a *dead body / police officer*.

2. A newspaper has different **sections**. This means it has different *colors / parts*.

3. If you **camp** somewhere, you stay there for a short time in a *hotel / tent*.

4. If something is **unlikely** to happen, you *think / don't think* it will happen.

5. If something is true **whatever** you may think, your opinion *makes no / can make a* difference.

WORD PARTS **C.** We can add *-ever* (meaning "any" or "every") to certain question words to form new words (e.g., **what** + *-ever* = **whatever**). Use the question words in the box to complete the sentences.

> **what**   **when**   **who**

1. Help yourself to _____**ever** you want from the fridge.
2. Can _____**ever** leaves last please lock the door?
3. Come over _____**ever** it's convenient for you—I'm free all day.

12B

SCANNING **A.** Read this timeline. What record did Amelia Earhart set?

Amelia Earhart *(1897–1937)*

1920: Attends an air show in California. Decides she wants to fly.

1921: Starts taking flying lessons. Becomes a pilot at age 24.

1932: Becomes the first woman to fly a plane alone across the Atlantic Ocean.

1937, May–June: Plans to be the first woman to fly a plane around the world. Flies with guide Fred Noonan across the U.S., south to Brazil, and across Africa, Asia, and Australia. They arrive in New Guinea on June 29.

1937, July 2: They head for an island in the Pacific, but are never seen again.

PREDICTING **B.** What do you think happened to Earhart and Noonan? Discuss with a partner. Then read the passage to check your ideas.

American pilot Linda Finch flies over Howland Island on a commemorative flight, retracing Amelia Earhart's 1937 route.

THE MISSING PILOT

A On July 2, 1937, Amelia Earhart and Fred Noonan left Lae, New Guinea, for Howland Island in the Pacific. This was without a doubt the longest and most dangerous part of their trip around the world. Earhart had trouble shortly after takeoff. The weather was stormy, so she had to fly at approximately 3,000 meters. Going this high, the plane used up gas quickly.

B After about 20 hours, Earhart and Noonan **approached** Howland Island. The island was only about a hundred kilometers away at this point, but the **bright** sun was **shining** in their faces, so they couldn't see it. Near Howland, a ship—the *Itasca*—was waiting. Earhart contacted the ship: "Gas is low," she said. The *Itasca* tried to maintain contact with her, but it got no **response**. Finally, the *Itasca* called for help. People searched for Earhart and Noonan for days. Despite great **efforts**, they found nothing.

EARHART'S 1937 FLIGHT ROUTE

Oakland, Calif.

PACIFIC OCEAN

Earhart and Noonan vanish

Lae

INDIAN OCEAN

— Flight path   - - Intended flight path

CLARE TRAINOR, ROSEMARY WARDLEY, NG STAFF. SOURCE: TIGHAR

Answers to a Mystery?

C What happened to Amelia Earhart? No one knows for sure. During the **flight**, she likely **headed** in the wrong direction because the sun was bright and it was hard to see. Perhaps she and Noonan got lost somewhere over the Pacific; soon after, her plane ran out of gas, and she **crashed** into the sea. Another idea is that Earhart might have landed on a nearby, uninhabited[1] island called Nikumaroro, where she later died. Researchers recently brought bone-sniffing dogs to the island, though, and no human bones were found. However, the dogs did detect[2] the smell of bones that decomposed[3] long ago—these bones could have been Earhart's. A more extreme theory is that Earhart flew the plane to the Japanese-controlled Marshall Islands, a thousand kilometers to the north, and later secretly returned to the United States under a new name.

D The first theory seems most likely. However, none of these ideas has been proven. Today, people are still **investigating** Earhart's and Noonan's **disappearance**. Whatever happened, Earhart probably died as she wished. "When I go," she once said, "I'd like best to go in my plane."

---

1 If a place is **uninhabited**, it has no people.

2 If you **detect** something, you find it or discover that it is present somewhere.

3 When things such as dead plants or animals **decompose**, they are slowly broken down into simpler parts or substances by natural processes.

A. Choose the best answer for each question.

GIST **1.** What could be another title for this reading?

    a. Pilot Mystery Is Finally Solved

    b. What Happened to Amelia Earhart?

    c. America's First Female Pilot

DETAIL **2.** According to the reading, why was flying to Howland Island difficult?

    a. Noonan didn't have a map.

    b. Their plane was damaged.

    c. Howland Island was very far from New Guinea.

DETAIL **3.** Shortly after taking off from New Guinea, what happened?

    a. The *Itasca* made contact with Earhart and Noonan.

    b. Earhart and Noonan tried to land on the *Itasca*.

    c. A storm forced Earhart and Noonan to fly higher.

VOCABULARY **4.** Which of these words or phrases is most similar in meaning to *ran out of* in paragraph C?

    a. removed

    b. filled up with

    c. had no more of

INFERENCE **5.** In paragraph D, when Earhart says "When I go …," what does *go* mean?

    a. fly

    b. die

    c. leave

A jar of face cream was found on Nikumaroro. This jar may have belonged to Amelia Earhart.

MATCHING **B.** Match each place with the correct description.

1. Nikumaroro •

2. New Guinea •

3. Howland Island •

4. Marshall Islands •

• a. where Earhart and Noonan last took off from

• b. where Earhart and Noonan were heading

• c. where some people believe Earhart flew to before returning to the U.S.

• d. where dogs have recently picked up the smell of human bones

Recognizing Degrees of Certainty

It is important to recognize how sure an author is about any claims that are made in a text. A fact would have a very high degree of certainty. Theories or speculations would have a lower degree of certainty. The following words and phrases can indicate degrees of certainty.

Complete certainty: *certainly, definitely, without a doubt, for sure, certain*

Strong certainty: *probably, likely*

Less certainty: *might, may, could, possibly, perhaps, maybe, doubtful*

IDENTIFYING **A.** Look at the sentences below (1–6) from Reading B. Underline the words and phrases that indicate degrees of certainty.

ANALYZING **B.** For each claim below, circle the author's degree of certainty (1 = lowest degree of certainty; 5 = highest degree of certainty). Then compare answers with a partner.

1. This was without a doubt the longest and most dangerous part of their trip around the world.   1   2   3   4   5

2. During the flight, she likely headed in the wrong direction because the sun was bright and it was hard to see.   1   2   3   4   5

3. Perhaps she and Noonan got lost somewhere over the Pacific.   1   2   3   4   5

4. Another idea is that Earhart might have landed on a nearby, uninhabited island called Nikumaroro, where she later died.   1   2   3   4   5

5. These bones could have been Earhart's.   1   2   3   4   5

6. Whatever happened, Earhart probably died as she wished.   1   2   3   4   5

CRITICAL THINKING Evaluating Theories   Discuss these questions with a partner.

▶ Look back at Reading B. Of the theories about Amelia Earhart's disappearance, which does the author think is most likely?

Theory: _____

▶ Do you agree with the author? What do you think happened to Earhart and Noonan? Note your answers below. Then compare them with your ideas in Before You Read B (on page 166).

_____

_____

COMPLETION **A.** Circle the correct words to complete the paragraph below.

Jim Thompson was an American businessman who helped revive Thailand's silk industry in the 1950s and 1960s. On March 26, 1967, while on vacation in Malaysia's Cameron Highlands, Thompson ¹**investigated / headed** out alone for an afternoon walk. He was never seen again. A huge search ²**effort / disappearance** was conducted, but no trace of him was found. After a(n) ³**investigation / flight**, the conclusion was that he fell into an animal trap or was eaten by a tiger. However,

△ **The last photo taken of Jim Thompson before he disappeared in 1967**

other theories have since been put forward. Some people believe he was murdered, while others think he faked his own death. His ⁴**disappearance / response** may remain a mystery forever. However, Thompson's presence can still be felt in Thailand today. Shoppers crowd his stores to buy ⁵**flight / bright** silk scarves and elegant ties, and his former home in Bangkok is a popular tourist attraction.

WORDS IN CONTEXT **B.** Complete the sentences. Circle the correct words.

1. Something that **shines** is *bright and clear / dull and dirty*.

2. If a plane **crashes**, it *takes off quickly / hits the ground or sea hard*.

3. A person who is taking a **flight** needs to go to the *airport / train station*.

4. When you **approach** something, you *get closer to / walk away from* it.

5. A **response** is a(n) *wish or need / answer or reply*.

WORD PARTS **C.** We can add the prefix *dis-* to some words to show an opposite meaning (e.g., *dis-* + *appear* = **disappear**). Complete the sentences using the words in the box. One word is extra.

ability	appear	approve	like

1. Although he is blind, he doesn't consider his lack of sight a **dis**_____.
2. Chemistry is the only subject I **dis**_____ at school.
3. The moon will **dis**_____ behind the clouds in a few minutes.

EARHART MYSTERY

Visitors attend the Amelia Earhart exhibit at the National Air and Space Museum in Washington, D.C.

BEFORE YOU WATCH

PREVIEWING   **A.** Read the extracts from the video. Match the words in **bold** with their definitions (1–5).

"As she approached, she landed on a **reef** and then went to the island. Earhart and Noonan waited for help to come, but … died of **thirst**."

"… the idea that Earhart was taken **prisoner** by the Japanese is supported by many people …"

"Some believe she was actually an American **spy**. Earhart's mission? To **pretend** she was having problems with her plane, so she would then have to fly to the Marshall Islands."

1. _____ : the feeling that you need to drink something
2. _____ : a person who secretly collects and reports information
3. _____ : a person who has been caught by an enemy (e.g., in war)
4. _____ : to behave as if something is true when you know that it is not
5. _____ : a long line of rocks, the top of which is just below or above the sea

COMPLETION **A.** Look at the chart below. What do you think the missing words are? Watch the video and complete the chart.

Theories	What happened to Amelia Earhart?
• "Crash and Sink" Theory	flew toward Howland Island → ran out of [1]_____ → plane crashed and sank
• Gardner Island Theory	flew to Gardner Island (now called Nikumaroro) → no [2]_____ → died of thirst
• A Prisoner of War	flew to Marshall Islands → captured by the Japanese → [3]_____ while being held prisoner
• An American Spy	flew to Marshall Islands to give the U.S. Navy a [4]_____ to search the area
• The Irene Bolam Connection	returned to the U.S. → lived as a [5]_____ in New Jersey under a new name

CRITICAL THINKING Reflecting

▶ The idea that Amelia Earhart was a spy is an example of a conspiracy theory (a belief that an event or situation is the result of a secret plan made by powerful people). Can you think of any other conspiracy theories? Note your ideas and share them with a partner.

_____

_____

▶ Why do you think some people believe in conspiracy theories? Are there any that you believe in? Discuss with a partner.

VOCABULARY REVIEW

Do you remember the meanings of these words? Check (✓) the ones you know. Look back at the unit and review any words you're not sure of.

Reading A

☐ achieve*   ☐ camp   ☐ evidence*   ☐ path   ☐ prove

☐ section*   ☐ suffer   ☐ unfortunately   ☐ unlikely   ☐ whatever

Reading B

☐ approach*   ☐ bright   ☐ crash   ☐ disappearance   ☐ effort

☐ flight   ☐ head   ☐ investigate*   ☐ response*   ☐ shine

* Academic Word List

Photo and Illustration Credits

Text Credits

Turn the Tide on Plastic. Here's How," by Laura Parker: NGM, Jun 2018, **161-162** Adapted from "Mystery on Everest," by Conrad Anker: NGM, Oct 1999, and "Out of Thin Air," by David Roberts: NGA, Fall 1999, **167** Adapted from "Amelia Earhart," by Virginia Morell: NGM, Jan 1998, and based on information from "Forensic Dogs Locate Spot Where Amelia Earhart May Have Died," by Rachel Hartigan Shea: news.nationalgeographic.com

NGK = National Geographic Kids
NGM = National Geographic Magazine
NGA = National Geographic Adventure

Acknowledgments

The Authors and Publisher would like to thank the following teaching professionals for their valuable feedback during the development of the series.

Akiko Hagiwara, Tokyo University of Pharmacy and Life Sciences; **Albert Lehner**, University of Fukui; **Alexander Cameron**, Kyushu Sangyo University; **Amira Traish**, University of Sharjah; **Andrés López**, Colégio José Max León; **Andrew Gallacher**, Kyushu Sangyo University; **Angelica Hernandez**, Liceo San Agustin; **Angus Painter**, Fukuoka University; **Anouchka Rachelson**, Miami Dade College; **Ari Hayakawa**, Aoyama Gakuin University; **Atsuko Otsuki**, Senshu University; **Ayako Hisatsune**, Kanazawa Institute of Technology; **Bogdan Pavliy**, Toyama University of International Studies; **Braden Chase**, The Braden Chase Company; **Brian J. Damm**, Kanda Institute of Foreign Languages; **Carol Friend**, Mercer County Community College; **Catherine Yu**, CNC Language School; **Chad Godfrey**, Saitama Medical University; **Cheng-hao Weng**, SMIC Private School; **Chisako Nakamura**, Ryukoku University; **Chiyo Myojin**, Kochi University of Technology; **Chris Valvona**, Okinawa Christian College; **Claire DeFord**, Olympic College; **Davi Sukses**, Sutomo 1; **David Farnell**, Fukuoka University; **David Johnson**, Kyushu Sangyo University; **Debbie Sou**, Kwong Tai Middle School; **Devin Ferreira**, University of Central Florida; **Eden Kaiser**, Framingham State University; **Ellie Park**, CNC Language School; **Elvis Bartra García**, Corporación Educativa Continental; **Emiko Yamada**, Westgate Corporation; **Eri Tamura**, Ishikawa Prefectural University; **Fadwa Sleiman**, University of Sharjah; **Frank Gutsche**, Tohoku University; **Frank Lin**, Guangzhou Tufu Culture; **Gavin Young**, Iwate University; **Gerry Landers**, GA Tech Language Institute; **Ghada Ahmed**, University of Bahrain; **Grace Choi**, Grace English School; **Greg Bevan**, Fukuoka University; **Gregg McNabb**, Shizuoka Institute of Science and Technology; **Helen Roland**, Miami Dade College; **Hiroshi Ohashi**, Kyushu University; **Hiroyo Yoshida**, Toyo University; **Hojin Song**, GloLink Education; **Jackie Bae**, Plato Language School; **Jade Wong**, Belilios Public School; **James McCarron**, Chiba University; **Jane Kirsch**, INTO George Mason University; **Jenay Seymore**, Hong Ik University; **John Appleby**, Kanda Institute of Foreign Languages; **John Nevara**, Kagoshima University; **Jonathan Bronson**, Approach International Student Center; **Joseph Zhou**, UUabc; **Junjun Zhou**, Menaul School; **Kaori Yamamoto**; **Katarina Zorkic**, Rosemead College; **Keiko Miyagawa**, Meiji University; **Kevin Tang**, Ritsumeikan Asia Pacific University; **Kieran Julian**, Kanda Institute of Foreign Languages; **Kim Kawashima**, Olympic College; **Kyle Kumataka**, Ritsumeikan Asia Pacific University; **Kyosuke Shimamura**, Kurume University; **Lance Stilp**, Ritsumeikan Asia Pacific University; **Li Zhaoli**, Weifang No.7 Middle School; **Liza Armstrong**, University of Missouri; **Lucas Pignolet**, Ritsumeikan Asia Pacific University; **Luke Harrington**, Chiba University; **M. Lee**, KCC; **Maiko Berger**, Ritsumeikan Asia Pacific University; **Mandy Kan**, CNEC Christian College; **Mari Nakamura**, English Square; **Masako Kikukawa**, Doshisha University; **Matthew Fraser**, Westgate Corporation; **Mayuko Matsunuma**, Seijo University; **Michiko Imai**, Aichi University; **Mei-ho Chiu**, Soochow University; **Melissa Potts**, ELS Berkeley; **Monica Espinoza**, Torrance Adult School; **Ms. Manassara Riensumettharadol**, Kasetsart University; **My Uyen Tran**, Ho Chi Minh City University of Foreign Languages and Information Technology; **Narahiko Inoue**, Kyushu University; **Neil Witkin**, Kyushu Sangyo University; **Olesya Shatunova**, Kanagawa University; **Patricia Fiene**, Midwestern Career College; **Patricia Nation**, Miami Dade College; **Patrick John Johnston**, Ritsumeikan Asia Pacific University; **Paul Hansen**, Hokkaido University; **Paula Snyder**, University of Missouri-Columbia; **Reiko Kachi**, Aichi University / Chukyo University; **Robert Dykes**, Jin-ai University; **Rosanna Bird**, Approach International Student Center; **Ryo Takahira**, Kurume Fusetsu High School; **Samuel Taylor**, Kyushu Sangyo University; **Sandra Stein**, American University of Kuwait; **Sara Sulko**, University of Missouri; **Serena Lo**, Wong Shiu Chi Secondary School; **Shin Okada**, Osaka University; **Silvana Carlini**, Colégio Agostiniano Mendel; **Silvia Yafai**, ADVETI: Applied Tech High School; **Stella Millikan**, Fukuoka Women's University; **Summer Webb**, University of Colorado Boulder; **Susumu Hiramatsu**, Okayama University; **Suzanne Littlewood**, Zayed University; **Takako Kuwayama**, Kansai University; **Takashi Urabe**, Aoyama-Gakuin University; **Teo Kim**, OROMedu; **Tim Chambers**; **Toshiya Tanaka**, Kyushu University; **Trevor Holster**, Fukuoka University; **Wakako Takinami**, Tottori University; **Wayne Malcolm**, Fukui University of Technology; **Wendy Wish**, Valencia College; **Xingwu Chen**, Xueersi-TAL; **Yin Wang**, TAL Education Group; **Yohei Murayama**, Kagoshima University; **Yoko Sakurai**, Aichi University; **Yoko Sato**, Tokyo University of Agriculture and Technology; **Yoon-Ji Ahn**, Daks Education; **Yu-Lim Im**, Daks Education; **Yuriko Ueda**, Ryukoku University; **Yvonne Hodnett**, Australian College of Kuwait; **Yvonne Johnson**, UWCSEA Dover

GLOSSARY

These words are used in *Reading Explorer* to describe various reading and critical thinking skills.

Analyze   to study a text in detail, e.g., to identify key points, similarities, and differences

Apply   to think about how an idea might be useful in other ways, e.g., solutions to a problem

Classify   to arrange things in groups or categories, based on their characteristics

Evaluate   to examine different sides of an issue, e.g., reasons for and against something

Infer   to "read between the lines"—information the writer expresses indirectly

Interpret   to think about what a writer means by a certain phrase or expression

Justify   to give reasons for a personal opinion, belief, or decision

Rank   to put things in order based on criteria, e.g., size or importance

Reflect   to think deeply about what a writer is saying and how it compares with your own views

Relate   to consider how ideas in a text connect with your own personal experience

Scan   to look through a text to find particular words or information

Skim   to look at a text quickly to get an overall understanding of its main idea

Summarize   to give a brief statement of the main points of a text

Synthesize   to use information from more than one source to make a judgment or comparison

INDEX OF EXAM QUESTION TYPES

The activities in *Reading Explorer, Third Edition* provide comprehensive practice of several question types that feature in standardized tests such as TOEFL® and IELTS.

Common Question Types	IELTS	TOEFL®	Page(s)
Multiple choice (gist, main idea, detail, reference, inference, vocabulary, paraphrasing)	✓	✓	10, 16, 25, 30, 39, 44, 53, 58, 67, 72, 81, 86, 95, 100, 107, 112, 121, 126, 135, 140, 149, 154, 163, 168
Completion (notes, diagram, chart)	✓		54, 59, 62, 67, 73, 82, 108, 135, 141, 144, 154, 164
Completion (summary)	✓	✓	39
Short answer	✓		53, 81, 101, 107, 122, 126
Matching headings / information	✓		17, 25, 58, 100, 168
Categorizing (matching features)	✓	✓	10, 16, 95, 163
True / False / Not Given	✓		30, 44, 72, 86, 140, 149
Rhetorical purpose		✓	30, 53, 58, 72, 86, 100, 107, 121, 140

The following tips will help you become a more successful reader.

1 Preview the text

Before you start reading a text, it's important to have some idea of the overall topic. Look at the title, photos, captions, and any maps or infographics. Skim the text quickly, and scan for any key words before reading in detail (see pages 11 and 31).

2 Use vocabulary strategies

Here are some strategies to use if you find a word or phrase you're not sure of:

- **Look for definitions** of new words within the reading passage itself (see page 101).
- **Identify the part of speech and use context** to guess the meaning of homonyms and new words (see pages 136 and 155).
- **Use a dictionary** if you need, but be careful to identify the correct definition.

3 Take notes

Note-taking helps you identify the main ideas and details within a text. It also helps you stay focused while reading. Try different ways of organizing your notes, and decide on a method that best suits you (see pages 108 and 127).

4 Infer information

Not everything is stated directly within a text. Use your own knowledge, and clues in the text, to make your own inferences and "read between the lines."

5 Make connections

As you read, look for words that help you understand how different ideas connect. For example:

- words that signal **reasons** (see page 45)
- words that indicate **sequence** (see pages 82 and 87)
- words that show degrees of **certainty** (see page 169)

6 Read critically

Ask yourself questions as you read a text. For example, if the author presents a point of view, are enough supporting reasons or examples provided? Is the evidence reliable? Does the author give a balanced argument? (see pages 59, 96, 164, and 169)

7 Create a summary

Creating a summary is a great way to check your understanding of a text. It also makes it easier to remember the main points. You can summarize in different ways based on the type of text. For example:

- **timelines or chain diagrams** (see page 82)
- **T-charts** (see pages 73 and 164)
- **Venn diagrams** (see page 163)
- **concept maps** (see page 54)
- **outline summaries** (see page 141)